The definitive, tried A–Z+ Impromptu speaking training, techniques, and strategies—guaranteed to help you unleash your God-given potential and dominate life's challenges.

Strategically Speaking for Success -

Think... Speak... DOMINATE

in 15 Seconds or Less!

by

Dr. Godfrey E. McAllister, DTM

"Doctor Perspective"

Think... Speak... Dominate in 15 Seconds or Less!

Publisher: GodWill Publishers

ISBN:

Printed in the USA

Cover/design/illustration credits: Doctor Perspective

For permissions, contact:

TSD15_Permissions@DoctorPerspective.com

Toastmasters International® and all other Toastmasters International trademarks and copyrights are the sole property of Toastmasters International. This book is the opinion of the author and is independent of Toastmasters International. It is not authorized by, endorsed by, sponsored by, affiliated with, or otherwise approved by Toastmasters International.

DEDICATION

Think... Speak... DOMINATE
In 15 Seconds or Less!

is dedicated to

Toastmasters International
on its Centenary Anniversary

Toastmasters International is a nonprofit educational organization that builds confidence and teaches public speaking skills through a worldwide network of clubs that meet online and in person. In a supportive community or corporate environment, members prepare and deliver speeches, respond to Impromptu questions, and give and receive constructive feedback.

It is through this regular practice that members are empowered to meet personal and professional communication goals. Founded in 1924, the organization is headquartered in Englewood, Colorado with over 265,000 members in more than 13,800 clubs in nearly 150 countries.

Contents

Chapter 6   77

The PREP and Beyond: Frameworks for Order Under Pressure 77

Chapter 7   87

Humor Without Risk: Wit That Wins, Not Wounds 87

Chapter 8   97

Mastering Transitions: Turning the Unexpected into Flow 97

Chapter 9   109

Voice, Tone, and the Music of Spontaneity 109

Chapter 13   161

High-Stakes Leadership Moments: Impromptu for Influence 161

Chapter 14   175

Handling the Curveball Question with Grace 175

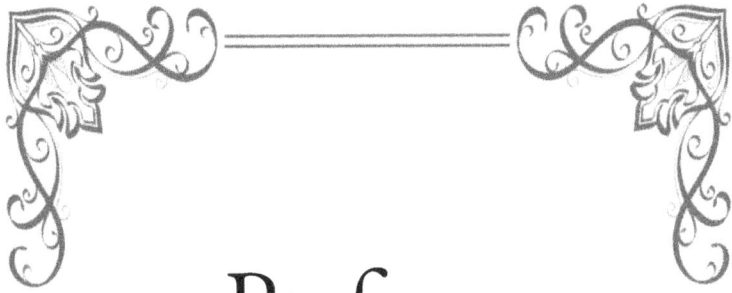

Preface

Think... Speak... Dominate in 15 Seconds or Less!

When the spotlight swings your way — in a meeting, at a dinner table, in a job interview, or on a stage — you rarely get to choose the timing, the topic, or the conditions.

But you always get to choose your response.

That moment — often no more than *fifteen seconds* — is a crossroads.

One path leads to stammering, filler words, and missed opportunity.

The other leads to clarity, connection, and influence that lingers long after the moment has passed.

This book is about mastering that second path.

Why Fifteen Seconds?

In every arena I've studied — politics, business, ministry, media — the first fifteen seconds of your response determine whether people will keep listening. Audiences, colleagues, and strangers alike make unconscious judgments in those opening moments. They decide whether you're worth their attention, whether you have credibility, and whether they trust you.

Fifteen seconds isn't just an arbitrary slice of time. It's the window where *perception is set* and *momentum is built*. Wait too long, and the moment moves on without you. Waste the opening, and your brilliance later may never be heard. But fill it with purpose, and you tilt the conversation in your favor — instantly.

My Journey to the Fifteen-Second Rule

I didn't arrive at this philosophy through theory. I earned it in the crucible of real-world speaking — from pulpits and boardrooms to competition stages and one-on-one encounters where every word counted. Over decades, I've seen people with flawless prepared speeches collapse when a question caught them off guard. I've also seen quiet, unassuming individuals seize a room's attention with a short, well-placed remark.

As a six-time multi-district ***Table Topics® Champion*** and a finalist in the ***World Championship of Public Speaking***, I've lived on both sides of that moment. I've felt the electric charge when a room leans in... and the weight of silence when I had nothing ready to say. What I discovered is this: Impromptu speaking is not an inborn talent. It's a skill — one you can learn, refine, and master.

What This Book Will Give You

This is not a book of gimmicks, "magic phrases," or one-size-fits-all templates. It is a ***system*** — grounded in psychology, refined in the crucible of my 24 years in the Toastmasters arena, and tested in professional, spiritual, and everyday contexts. You will learn:

How to think with precision under pressure.

How to organize your thoughts instantly using frameworks that work anywhere.

How to deliver responses that sound as prepared as your best keynote.

How to turn surprise questions into strategic opportunities.

How to dominate the room — without dominating people.

The methods here are not just for professional speakers. They are for *leaders, parents, pastors, entrepreneurs, teachers, students, and anyone who faces unscripted moments that matter*.

Why This Book is Different

Most public speaking books focus on prepared speeches. They treat Impromptu moments like side notes. This book reverses that. Here, Impromptu skill is not a bonus — it's the main event. Each chapter gives you tools you can apply *the same day you read them*. You'll see real-life case studies, step-by-step demonstrations, and practical exercises designed to create visible improvement within weeks — or even days.

In addition, you will find *Simulations* in each section — short, 1-2-minute examples that model exactly how to apply the principles. These are not hypotheticals; they are word-for-word responses you can study, adapt, and make your own.

Our "Bubbles" & "Practical Point to Ponder"

Every Chapter begins with some "bubbles" on the first page. These are selections of direct quotations from **Think... Speak... Dominate in 15 Seconds or Less!** Many of the quotations are in the current Chapter... some are not... but are somewhere in the book. Have some fun with them by trying to locate them. It will also be an excellent way to reinforce some of the things you will either learn about, or be reminded of in this book.

Think... Speak... Dominate in 15 Seconds or Less! is sprinkled with Practical Points to Ponder from thinkers and speakers of the past, and of course, Doctor Perspective! What communication connected practical point would you like the world to ponder. Share it with us.

Welcome to a world-wide community

When you purchase your personal copy of **Think... Speak... Dominate in 15 Seconds or Less!** you automatically have earned a seat in the World-wide Impromptu Speakers Empowerment (WISE) community. This membership is your ticket to scheduled webinars, as well as to discounts to our special events. Just send us a message at:

https://TheWISEworld.org

A Final Word Before We Begin

You may be reading this because you've been caught off guard before — and didn't like how it felt. Or maybe you've tasted the rush of owning the moment and want to do it again, every time. Either way, this book will equip you to walk into any room, face any question, and know that your next fifteen seconds can be your best.

Because when you can *think* with clarity, *speak* with purpose, and *dominate* the moment — even for just fifteen seconds — you change how people see you. More importantly, you change how you see yourself.

Let's begin!

❋❋❋❋❋❋❋❋❋❋— ♣ — ♣ —❋❋❋❋❋❋❋❋❋❋

Death and life are in the power of the tongue, and those who love it
will eat its fruits.
Proverbs 18:21

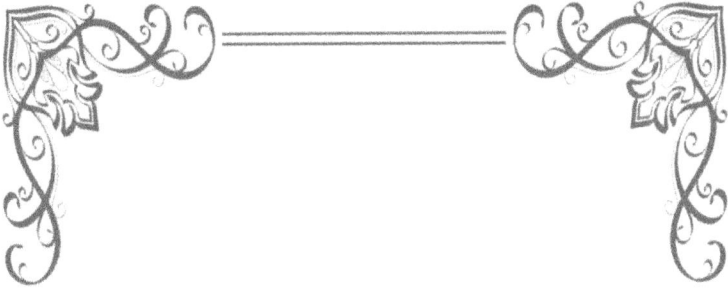

Chapter 1

My First Experience at a Toastmasters Meeting

Look out for...

1) *A good meeting inspires. A catalytic one transforms.*
2) *Fast thinking is a muscle—train it or trip over it.*
3) *What looks like blur is actually control repeated at speed.*
4) *Speed without wisdom is reckless.*
5) *Some soared. Some stumbled. All grew.*
6) *Skill compounds faster than you think when the reps are daily.*
7) *That's what a great first response feels like—coiled, balanced, directed*

♥ In the Beginning

I was hooked. Forty-eight hours after my very first Toastmasters meeting in 2001, I felt the strange ache of withdrawal. Not from coffee. From adrenaline, clarity, connection—whatever that rare compound is that floods your system when a room leans in and your words actually land. The meeting I'd attended at Pacesetters Toastmasters Club in Kingston Jamaica —the second-oldest club in the Caribbean—wasn't just "good." It was catalytic. People I had never met stood up, faced a friendly but demanding audience, and tried to build meaning in real time. Some soared. Some stumbled. All grew.

I walked in confident. By then I was a preacher—seasoned, Spirit-led, used to structuring a message—and a successful businessman whose insurance solution still generated income years later. But that night exposed an untrained muscle: the ability to think fast and speak clean when the topic, timing, and temperature weren't mine to choose. Toastmasters called it Table Topics®. In ministry I'd call it stewardship of the moment. In business I'd call it competitive advantage. Either way, I wanted it. I soon learned that fast thinking is a muscle—train it or trip over it

The Table Topics Master called my name. I stood, not quite sure why my legs felt lighter than they should. The prompt flashed like a camera bulb: "What would you do if you were invisible for one day?" No notes. No warm-up. No rescue.

I opened my mouth. "Umm... I'd go to my boss's office and find out why he's always giving me such a hard time." Laughter. Encouraging, energizing laughter. I leaned into it. "I'd also walk into the girls' locker room—but I'd keep my eyes closed—just to find out what it smells like." Louder laughter. I didn't win the ribbon. But I walked back to my seat with something far better than a ribbon: proof. Proof that I could be thrown into the deep end and still move water.

That night didn't crown me a champion. It baptized me as a beginner.

~~~~~~~~~~~~~~~ •••• •••• ~~~~~~~~~~~~~~~
"Speed without wisdom is reckless."
— **Doctor Perspective™**

Beginners get hungry. I went home and replayed everything—what worked, what wobbled, where I reached for humor because I didn't yet have a framework. By the next morning, I wasn't thinking about a single funny line; I was thinking about a repeatable way to make any first fifteen seconds count.

♥ The meeting that rewired my brain

Prepared messages had never frightened me. Give me a week, a Bible passage, a clean sheet, and I could build a strong sermon with structure, cadence, and call-to-action. But that night revealed a gap between prepared eloquence and real-time agility. Real life, unlike a pulpit schedule, doesn't respect your calendar. People interrupt. Reporters shove mics. Clients change scope mid-meeting. Children ask impossible questions at the worst possible time. If your influence depends on control, your influence will always be fragile.

Table Topics® introduced me to a new economy: clarity on demand. It also showed me something else—no one is born with this. Yes, some people are quick. Some have humor at their fingertips. But reliable, respectful, high-impact responses under pressure come from training, not temperament. I had training for pulpit work. I needed training for surprise work.

Two days after that first meeting, I wrote a simple sentence at the top of a notepad: "How to take off clean in 15 seconds." Under it, I jotted fragments from what I had seen and felt: connect to the moment; answer cleanly; give one reason or story; invite the next step. I didn't yet have names for the steps. I only had a sense that if I could make the first fifteen seconds strong, the next sixty would feel inevitable.

♥ What the first prompt actually taught me

"Invisible for a day" is a frivolous prompt—unless you listen to what it forces you to do. It compels you to choose a direction fast, or drown in possibilities. It tempts you toward a cheap laugh, or challenges you toward a meaningful insight. It reveals whether your instincts are to hide behind words, or to own a simple idea and carry it to a destination.

In that moment I stumbled onto three instincts that would later become deliberate habits:

Connection over content. I referenced a boss. Everyone in the room had one. Instantly we shared context.

Specific over vague. "Locker room" is concrete. Specificity paints a picture.

Closure over drift. Even a throwaway joke closes a loop. Closure signals control.

Those three instincts aren't enough to build a reputation on. But they're enough to survive your first minutes until you have a framework you can trust.

♥ Nature doesn't guess — neuroplasticity and myelin do the work

There's a reason your tenth Table Topics response feels steadier than your first: the brain changes with use. Myelin—the fatty sheath around neural pathways—thickens with correct repetition, insulating circuits so signals fire faster and cleaner. That's why a pianist's fingers "just know," or why a nurse can spike an IV bag while answering a question. The skill wasn't sprinkled on them. It was wrapped—layer by layer—in myelin through purposeful practice.

Think of a kingfisher diving at high speed into water. Its beak's shape minimizes splash and drag, allowing seamless entry. Engineers famously studied this to reduce noise on bullet trains. The kingfisher doesn't debate entry strategies; its design solves the problem at the speed of reality. In human communication, ***design*** is your mental framework. When surprise appears, you don't manufacture poise—you access design.

The first fifteen seconds: what I wish I had known that night

If I could rewind to that exact prompt and give my younger self one page of notes, it would say: "In your first sentence, prove you heard the question

◇ ♦ ◇ ♦ ◇— ♣— ♣—◇ ♦ ◇ ♦ ◇— ♣— ♣—◇ ♦ ◇ ♦ ◇

"I never could make a good impromptu speech without several hours to prepare it."

— Mark Twain

and that you're safe to listen to; in your second, answer in one clause; in your third, justify with one story, reason, or picture; in your fourth, invite a next step." Later I would call that sequence ***Anchor, Answer, Advance, Ask***. In that order, it is astonishingly reliable. In a later chapter we'll dissect it in full. Here, I want you to feel how it changes the same moment:

"Fascinating question." (Anchor—signals listening and buys micro-seconds)

"If I were invisible for a day, I would go where decisions are made." (Answer—one clause)

"I'd sit in on a negotiation to learn how real power behaves when it thinks no one is watching." (Advance—one reason/story)

"Where would you go if no one could see you?" (Ask—turns monologue into dialogue)

Do you lose the laugh? Maybe. Do you gain credibility? Almost certainly. When you are building a career on trust, credibility beats a cheap laugh every day of the week.

Real-world pressure: a finance director, a tough room, and a better first line

A finance director I coached had a recurring nightmare: the CEO ends a slide deck with, "Okay, why should we trust these numbers after last quarter?" His instinct was to apologize, explain, and then drown everyone in detail. We re-trained the first fifteen seconds.

"Fair question, especially after Q2." (Anchor)

"We revised the model to use three-year rolling trends instead of single-year snapshots." (Answer)

"That change reduces the weight of outliers and would have corrected last quarter's miss by 80 basis points." (Advance)

"Would you like me to show the side-by-side?" (Ask)

Two sentences into that answer, the room's shoulders went down. Not because the math changed, but because the ***mindset*** changed: calm, competent, collaborative.

Science in your bloodstream: the cheetah's start isn't chaos

Watch a cheetah accelerate. It doesn't flail. It coils, balances, and then releases force along a line. The tail counters torque. The spine stores and returns energy. What looks like blur is actually ***control*** repeated at speed. That's what a great first response feels like—coiled, balanced, directed. You're not "winging it." You're releasing trained control across a short distance.

Simulation 1: "They just cut our budget—say something encouraging"

Context: You're a department lead. Minutes before your all-hands, you learn your budget was trimmed 12%. Your team is anxious. You have to address them without notes.

"Before we talk numbers, I want to acknowledge what you're feeling."
"We lost twelve percent of our budget this morning."
"Here's how we'll respond: we'll protect the core work that serves our clients, we'll pause two low-impact experiments, and we'll get creative about partnerships to multiply what remains. We've done more with less before, and our mission did not shrink twelve percent today."
"I'll open the floor for concerns, and I'd also like to hear your best ideas for low-cost, high-impact wins this quarter."

That's roughly two minutes when delivered at a measured pace. It validates, informs, focuses, and invites. No spin. No panic. Clear next steps. Your people don't need perfection. They need posture.

♥ From laughter to lessons:
humility, respect, and the line you don't cross

About that locker-room quip. Did it work that night? Yes. Would I use it now? No. Speed without wisdom is reckless. Early in your journey you will say things that land but do not build you. The rule I teach now: ***Humor must never purchase approval at the expense of respect.*** If

"Theory is only as powerful as practice."
— Doctor Perspective™

your joke undermines the dignity of anyone in the room (or anyone not in the room), the short-term laugh will become a long-term liability.

Leadership in microphone moments requires a second internal filter: "Will I be glad this sentence is quoted with my name on it?" If the answer is "maybe not," choose a different sentence. Influence accumulates; so, do regrets.

♥ The habit that multiplies everything: after-action review

Pilots debrief. Athletes watch film. Surgeons review complications. Great Impromptu speakers do after-action review, even if it's sixty silent seconds on the drive home. Ask four questions:

What actually happened? (Not the story you wish happened—the tape-accurate version.)

What worked? (Name it. Keep it.)

What failed? (Name it without shame.)

What will I do differently next time? (One concrete tweak.)

That four-question loop is like adding rings to a tree. Each cycle thickens your trunk. Over months, your presence changes shape.

Nature's reminder: the bamboo's roots and the snow leopard's restraint

You've heard the bamboo story: years of invisible roots, weeks of visible rise. Pair it with the snow leopard. It doesn't sprint after every goat. It chooses. Conservation of effort is part of its power. Your speaking life will tempt you to "say more" when the right answer is "say less, better." Roots plus restraint. Depth plus decision. Those two instincts—grow and choose—make you dangerous in the best sense of the word.

Simulation 2: "Q&A turns hostile—answer without heat"

Context: You present a proposal. A stakeholder snaps: "This is just spin. Why should we waste budget on your plan?"

"I hear the frustration behind that, and I appreciate the candor."
"The plan looks like spin if it can't produce measurable outcomes in ninety

days."

"Here are the two metrics we're staking this on: cost per qualified lead, and cycle time from first contact to close. If those don't improve by the targets we've set, we sunset the initiative. No sunk-cost loyalty."

"Would it help if I walk through the exact triggers that would shut this down so you can see the guardrails we built?"

Notice the heat leaves the room when you name tests that could prove you wrong. Courage isn't bulldozing; it's inviting accountability in public.

A pastor's curveball
and the ministry version of real-time clarity

A young associate pastor in Lagos told me about a Sunday when a visiting speaker canceled minutes before service. The senior pastor looked at him: "Son, bring us the Word." Heart pounding, he walked up and said, "Family, we didn't plan this. God did." He read Luke 18:1 and built a five-minute exhortation on prayer that was simple, scriptural, and strong. He didn't exhale eloquence. He applied structure: anchor the moment, answer with a single truth, advance with one Scripture and one story, ask for a response. People remember his composure more than his outline. Sometimes your first fifteen seconds are the whole sermon.

Science illustration: working memory is a desk—clear it quickly

Working memory is like a small desk where you arrange the papers you need right now. Under pressure, that desk gets cluttered with self-talk, fear, and the noise of a room. The fastest way to make space is to ***name the moment*** out loud ("That's a fair question," "This is difficult news," "I wasn't expecting that, but here's what I can say with confidence"). Naming the moment is like swiping everything nonessential off the desk. You can now fit a single clear sentence and the one support that matters.

The day-to-day drills that forge the public moments

Not every rep has a microphone. Most don't. Try these daily drills:

One-breath answers. A family member asks a question; answer what was asked in a single breath. It forces concision.

Three-word summaries. After listening to someone, summarize their point in three words. It trains distillation.

Headline then detail. When someone asks for input, give the headline first ("Short version: we should delay by one week"), then one reason. It trains order.

These drills seem small. They are, until you multiply them by thirty days. Skill compounds faster than you think when the reps are daily.

Simulation 3: "Offer comfort—no clichés, no notes"

Context: A community vigil after a tragic accident. You are called up without warning to say a few words.

"We gather with heavy hearts, and I will not pretend words can carry all this weight."
"But grief is not a sign that we lack faith; it's a sign that we loved and were loved. If you didn't love, you wouldn't hurt."
"Here is what we can do tonight: we can say the names out loud; we can hold one another without rushing; and we can commit to be here again next week—not just tonight—because grief is a marathon, not a speech."
"If you need someone to stand with you in the days ahead, look around. You are not alone. We are not going anywhere."

Two minutes. No platitudes. Dignity, presence, promise.

♥ Mistakes I made so you don't have to

I made all of these:

Over-explaining. I thought more words equaled more persuasion. It equals fatigue.

※※※※※※※※※※—✤—✤—※※※※※※※※※※

"Plans are worthless, but planning is everything."
— Dwight D. Eisenhower

Performing humility. "I'm probably not the best person..." taught the room to doubt me. Real humility requires having value to offer, and effectively delivering it with clarity and sincerity.

Chasing laughs. A laugh bought at the price of someone's dignity invoices you later with interest.

Answering the wrong question. Listening lazily wastes your only currency—attention.

Dodging asks. Good answers invite next steps. Fear avoids them. Leaders make asks.

The table you can carry into any room

Carry this mental cheat sheet until it's muscle memory:

Anchor the moment: "That's fair," "I hear you," "Let's name what just happened."

Answer in one clause. If your sentence needs commas, you're probably saying two things. Pick one.

Advance with one proof: a story, statistic, reason, analogy, or Scripture.

Ask for the next step: a decision, a follow-up, a reflection, a small action.

When you feel scrambled, touch each corner in order. That's your portable stage.

A nature/science double: murmuration and murmurs

Watch a murmuration of starlings—thousands move like a single organism, adjusting in split-seconds without colliding. Scientists call it "scale-free correlation." Each bird attends to a small number of neighbors, not the whole cloud. Under pressure, do the same: don't attend to every face. Choose three—one friendly, one neutral, one skeptical—and let your eye contact orbit them. That small pattern will steer the whole room.

Now the cardiac echo: a heart murmur is turbulence when blood flow is

~~~~~~~~~~~~~ •••• •••• ~~~~~~~~~~~~~
"If I am to speak for ten minutes, I need a week for preparation; if an hour, I am ready now."

— Woodrow Wilson

disrupted. You fix it by repairing structure, not by willing the noise away. If your answers sound noisy, you don't need courage first—you need structure.

Action steps you can complete this week

Find a live rep. Attend one Toastmasters meeting or any Impromptu Speech Club. Volunteer once.

Film one response. Your phone is a coach. Watch for your first sentence, your last sentence, and whether you invited anything.

Build one vault page. Start a single document titled "Two-minute stories." Add five true, short stories from your life with one line about the lesson in each.

Practice one ask. End one meeting this week with a clear, respectful request: "By Friday 3 PM, please send me one risk you see and one idea you'd try."

What changed between that first meeting and everything after

I did not get smarter. I got simpler. I stopped trying to impress and started trying to serve the moment with the best sentence I could find in the time I had. I stopped confusing speed with value. I learned that **clean beats clever** and **kind beats cutting**—especially when a room is tense. I layered practice like myelin layers a nerve. I competed, won, lost, debriefed, coached, learned, and repeated. The awards were nice. The transformation was better: I no longer feared the unexpected question. I started to welcome it.

Call to action

You don't need a stage to begin. You need a moment—and you will have one today. When the question comes, breathe once and do four things in order: Anchor. Answer. Advance. Ask. Then write down what happened and what you'll change next time. Repeat that cycle for thirty days and you will feel your mental feet under you in every room you enter.

The night I first stood for Table Topics® did not certify me. It called me. If this chapter calls you, answer it out loud. Your next fifteen seconds are not a trap; they are a test you can pass. Choose your first sentence on purpose. The room will feel it. More importantly, so will you.

JOURNAL
Write it Down Before It Escapes!

◇ ◆ ◇ ◆ ◇ — ♣ — ♣ — ◇ ◆ ◇ ◆ ◇ — ♣ — ♣ — ◇ ◆ ◇ ◆ ◇

"Not every curveball deserves a full swing."

— Doctor Perspective™

Chapter 2

The 15-Second Window

Look out for...

8) *You are setting the frame through which every subsequent word will be judged.*

9) *Biology helps you here: myelination—the insulation around neural pathways—thickens with repetition, speeding signals.*

10) *"What will change?" is what stumbles mean.*

11) *Clarity is kindness. Specificity is respect. Both belong in the first moments.*

12) *Anchor the moment. Answer the core. Advance with one vivid fact. Ask to engage.*

13) *Your calibrated tone plus a second ask creates conversational resonance—small prompts that amplify shared purpose.*

♥ Why the first moments decide everything

You have far less time than you think. When the light finds you, when the question lands, when the room turns and waits—your listener's brain is already sorting: safe/unsafe, clear/unclear, relevant/irrelevant. In those first breaths you are not merely "starting"—you are **setting** the frame through which every subsequent word will be judged. Call it the 15-Second Window: a brief, volatile space in which attention is won or lost, trust is extended or withheld, and momentum either clicks into gear or stalls where it stands.

This window is not a trick of performance; it is a fact of cognition. Humans "thin-slice"—we form fast, sticky impressions from minimal data. Voice timbre, micro-expressions, posture, first phrasing: these are not cosmetic; they are diagnostic signals your listener reads before your content has a chance to argue for itself. The gift is that you can design those signals. With the right preparation and habits, your 15 seconds can consistently buy you the next 60, then the next five minutes, then the decision that changes the room.

Consider the quiet power of an ER triage nurse. A patient arrives, chaotic and loud. The nurse meets them with steady eyes, an even voice, and a sentence that anchors the moment: "You're with me now—we're going to handle this." The words are simple; the first seconds carry authority. That is the same physics of attention you carry to the lectern, the client call, the family conversation at a kitchen table: presence first, then content.

♥ What the brain is doing while you start talking

Three filters fire almost instantly: **competence**, **character**, and **connection**.

Competence: Do you sound like you know what you're doing? Your pace, diction, and first verb signal mastery or muddle.

Character: Do you feel trustworthy? Warmth without flattery, calm without indifference.

Connection: Do you appear to understand *this* audience and *this* moment? Relevance is not a tag at the end; it's a scent in the first sentence.

A nature picture helps: migrating geese test the wind in micro-adjustments before committing to a formation. They don't "hope" the air will carry them; they *sample* it, then lock in. Listeners do the same. Your opening gives them wind to fly with—or turbulence to flee.

Practical implication: your first sentence should **reduce uncertainty** and **increase perceived value**. Reduce uncertainty by naming the moment ("You're wondering if this change helps or hurts—here's the short answer"). Increase value by previewing payoff ("In two minutes you'll know how to explain this to your team"). Clarity is kindness. Specificity is respect. Both belong in second one.

♥ The AAA-A engine: Anchor, Answer, Advance, Ask

You need a reliable ignition sequence. The AAA-A engine works under pressure because it maps to how people think.

Anchor the moment: show you see what they see.
Answer the core question plainly.
Advance with one vivid fact, example, or reason.
Ask to engage and direct the next step.

Corporate scene: "That's the question on everyone's mind. Sales dipped because our primary supplier missed two shipments. We added a backup vendor last week—inventory risk is now halved. Would it help to see the revised timeline before we vote?"

Ministry scene: "Many of us walked in carrying a private weight. The text today is short, but it lifts heavier than you think. It shows how God meets people mid-journey. Can we look at the first line together?"

Family scene: "We're both tired and we want the same thing—a weekend

———✦——✦——ẽ ẽ ẽẽ ẽ ẽ——✦——✦———

"Where observation is concerned, chance favours only the prepared mind."

— **Louis Pasteur**

without tension. The plan I'm suggesting saves Saturday morning for rest and still gets the errands done. If we try it for two weeks, will you tell me what worked and what didn't?"

In each case the window is used not to impress but to orient. That is the true business of the first seconds: alignment.

♥ Frameworks you can grab in real time

Your opening sequence gets you rolling; you still need a road to travel. Under time pressure, choose a simple frame so your listener's working memory doesn't drown.

PREP (Point–Reason–Example–Point)
Point: "Respect beats popularity for leaders."
Reason: "Respect is built on consistency and fairness."
Example: "A shift manager who enforces rules evenly gets cooperation even from critics."
Point: "Be liked if you can, but be reliable first."

PCS (Problem–Cause–Solution) for practical issues
Problem: "Our response times slipped."
Cause: "Hand-offs between teams create dead zones."
Solution: "A shared queue and a daily 10-minute standup."

PPF (Past–Present–Future) for change and vision
Past: "We trained speakers to memorize."
Present: "Now we train them to modularize ideas."
Future: "Tomorrow's standout is the one who can remix insight live."

SCQA (Situation–Complication–Question–Answer) for persuasion
Situation: "We've grown 40%."
Complication: "Our processes didn't."
Question: "How do we scale without losing soul?"
Answer: "Automate the repetitive; ritualize the relational."

A science parallel: octopuses solve mazes by testing paths quickly and discarding the dead ends. A simple frame is your neural maze—less time deciding the route, more time moving through it. When in doubt, default to PREP; it's concise, listener-friendly, and impossible to get lost in.

♥ Nonverbal leadership in fifteen seconds

You can say "I'm confident" with words; your body can contradict you. Align them.

Posture: imagine a string lifting the crown of your head. Ground your feet. Unlock the knees.

Breath: inhale low, release slow. Your voice rides air; manage the air and you manage the sound.

Eye contact: triangular—left, right, center—so no one feels invisible and you never tunnel into a single face.

Gesture: purposeful, near the midline, palms occasionally visible (it telegraphs honesty).

Pace: conversational, not performative; speed up on narrative, slow on conclusions; pause one beat before your hook and one beat after.

Picture a red-tailed hawk banking in a crosswind. The wings don't flap harder; they angle smarter. That's nonverbal management: fewer, cleaner adjustments create a feeling of quiet command. Your first fifteen seconds should look like that—composed enough to calm the room, alive enough to energize it.

◇ ♦ ◇ ♦ ◇ — ♣ — ♣ — ◇ ♦ ◇ ♦ ◇ — ♣ — ♣ — ◇ ♦ ◇ ♦ ◇

"A well-timed pause is the secret sauce of humor."
— Doctor Perspective™

♥ When the window opens hostile

Sometimes the first sound you hear is dissent. If you react to tone instead of content, you forfeit the frame. Use a three-move response: ***Name, Neutralize, Navigate***.

Name the emotion without labeling the person: "I can hear the frustration."

Neutralize with a limiting agreement: "You're right about the timeline slipping."

Navigate to the path forward: "Here's what changed last week and what we need from this group to finish by Friday."

Think of judo. You don't meet force with force; you redirect it into motion that serves your aim. In language, that is the respectful acknowledgment that keeps a window open long enough to repair trust.

Simulation 1 - Impromptu Question

Prompt: *"A change you resisted at first but now appreciate."*

"I was certain the new feedback ritual would waste time. Five minutes at the end of every meeting felt like five minutes less for 'real work.' The first week, I treated it like a box to tick: polite comments, vague praise, a quick exit. Then something happened. A junior analyst said, 'I'm confused about who owns decisions after we leave this room.' Nobody had named it. We all felt it. The next day we drew a one-page 'decision map'—who consults, who decides, who informs. Two weeks later, meetings were shorter and follow-through doubled. The ritual I resisted exposed a friction I had learned to ignore. I thought feedback would slow us; it sped us. I thought it would bruise egos; it built them. So, if you see me guarding my calendar, remind me of this: five minutes is a small price for the clarity that saves five hours tomorrow. I didn't need another meeting. I needed a mirror. Now, when the timer chimes for feedback, I'm the first to say, 'Let's look—because what we see together, we can fix together.'"

Notice the AAA-A bones are still visible: anchored context, clear answer, a single developed example, and an implicit ask ("remind me... let's look..."). That's deliberate. Under pressure, skeletons carry you.

♥ From nerves to fuel

Anxiety is data. It means the moment matters. Your body is lending you resources—oxygenation, alertness, speed. The winning move is *relabeling*: not "I'm anxious," but "I'm mobilized." Perform a 20-second reset: feet grounded, inhale four counts, hold two, exhale six. As the exhale lengthens, the vagus nerve down-shifts your system.

Pair this physiology with a mental script: "Name, claim, aim." Name the state ("energy"), claim the purpose ("to serve clarity"), aim the action ("answer in one sentence, then advance").

Consider the cheetah: the heart rate spikes *before* the sprint. That surge is not panic; it is preparation. The cheetah does not apologize for its pulse. Neither should you.

♥ Story power inside the window

A micro-story buys attention ethically. Keep it under two sentences to start, with a sensory anchor and a pivot.

Sensory anchor: "The room smelled like fresh paint and fear."

Pivot to point: "We were about to announce a change that would save money and cost comfort."

Or: "At 3 a.m. the ICU monitor pinged; the nurse didn't look scared, so I decided not to be." Pivot: "Confidence is contagious; lend it with your first breath."

Why stories? The brain knits narrative into memory more readily than naked facts. Bees dance to tell other bees where nectar lives; the hive remembers and acts. Your first two sentences can be a dance that points the room toward value.

※※※※※※※※※※— ♣ — ♣ —※※※※※※※※※※

"Plans are worthless, but planning is everything."
— **Dwight D. Eisenhower**

Simulation 2 – Impromptu Question

Prompt: *"Is speed or accuracy more important?"*

"Speed without accuracy is motion without meaning; accuracy without speed is truth that arrives too late. Picture a fire department. If the trucks roll fast to the wrong address, the house still burns. If the crew waits for perfect information, the house still burns. The leaders I admire train for what I call 'decisive accuracy'—fast enough to matter, careful enough to trust. Here's how that looks in a day: we prepare templates for common scenarios so we don't reinvent the wheel. We write one clear sentence before we write a paragraph so our aim is visible. And we build a culture where the first draft is welcomed and the second draft is expected. When seconds matter, we move; when minutes appear, we refine; when hours are available, we rehearse. Ask a pilot on final approach whether speed or accuracy comes first. They'll tell you: 'Neither. Alignment does.' In work and in life, alignment is knowing what matters most and pointing your first words there. So, when the next urgent decision finds you, take the beat that buys accuracy, then move at the speed that honors the moment. That balance will save more houses than either virtue alone."

Note the hinge: "alignment." Your 15-second open should always name the hinge virtue and steer there.

Advanced upgrades: calibration, stacking, and the second ask

Three master moves deepen your influence once you're through the gate.

Calibration: match tone to the room's emotional baseline, then guide it. A grieving congregation does not need your thunder in second one; it needs your presence.

Stacking: add one well-chosen statistic or analogy to fortify a claim without drowning it. "We cut onboarding time by 37%" lands harder than "a lot faster."

Second Ask: after your initial AAA-A, return with a micro-question to confirm traction. "Does that align with your concern?" Agreement is glue.

A physics echo: resonance occurs when an external frequency matches a system's natural frequency, amplifying the signal. Your calibrated tone plus a second ask creates conversational resonance—small prompts that amplify shared purpose.

Practicing like a pro: build the reflex

Skills you can't access in pressure aren't skills; they're trivia. Practice must mimic stress to wire the reflex.

Hot-seat drills: friends or colleagues rapid-fire prompts. You answer in 30 seconds using AAA-A + PREP or PCS. Rotate roles.

Constraint sprints: answer with exactly two sentences; then answer with exactly one minute; then answer with a headline and three bullets.

Rehearsed spontaneity: maintain a "story bank" (one-paragraph scenes from work, family, faith, and nature) tagged by theme (risk, change, mercy, growth). In the wild, you're never truly "off-the-cuff"; you're recombining banked elements.

Biology helps you here: myelination—the insulation around neural pathways—thickens with repetition, speeding signals. Reps make fast, clean retrieval possible. That feeling of "flow" in the first fifteen seconds is not magic; it is myelin.

Simulation 3 - Impromptu Question

Prompt: *"What does respect look like when you disagree?"*

"Respect, to me, is how we hold the person when we cannot hold their position. It sounds like this: 'I can see why you'd want that outcome; here's why I can't support it—and here's what I can support.' It looks like this: square shoulders, steady eye contact, voice low enough to suggest you're here to solve, not to score. Last year a partner pushed for a launch date I believed would risk quality. I wanted to win the point; I decided to win the relationship. I opened with our shared aim: 'We both want trust on day one.' I named the risk without naming blame: 'If we ship early, our first reviews may train

"The pause is not hesitation; it is orchestration."

— **Doctor Perspective™**

the market to doubt us.' I offered a path that preserved urgency and integrity: 'Let's pilot with fifty customers, harvest feedback for two weeks, and launch to the list with proof instead of promises.' We did—and our open rates doubled. Here's what I learned: agreement is nice, alignment is better, and alignment is built in the way we begin. So, when your next disagreement comes, carry your respect into the first fifteen seconds like a gift. People remember how you made them feel at hello long after they forget who was technically right."

♥ Putting it all together: a model open you can adapt

You can draft a versatile universal opener and tune it on the fly:

Name the now: "You're weighing speed against safety, and the clock is loud."

Answer in a sentence: "We'll keep speed by simplifying decisions and keep safety by testing in small loops."

Advance with proof: "Two teams did this last quarter; cycle time dropped 28% with zero defects."

Ask: "Shall I walk you through the three loops and who owns each?"

Note how little drama you need. The dignity of clarity persuades.

Troubleshooting the first fifteen seconds

If you blank: say what you *do* know. "Here's what is clear today..." Then ask a clarifier that buys you five more seconds: "Is the priority cost or speed?" Answer either path.

If you ramble: stop, breathe, and meta-signal the reset. "Let me put this in a clean frame." Then deploy PREP.

If you're interrupted: treat it as collaboration, not conflict. "Jumping in is helpful—are you asking about timing or budget?" Narrow, then respond.

If you mis-speak: correct cleanly without drama. "Let me correct that figure: 18%, not 8." Continue.

In ecology, disturbances (a fallen tree, a small fire) can renew a forest; handled deliberately, your own "disturbances" can renew credibility rather than destroy it.

♥ Applications beyond the stage

Interviews: The dreaded "Tell me about yourself" is a gift if you treat it as a 15-second frame. "I help teams turn ambiguity into action. In my last role we cut cycle time 22% by clarifying decisions and automating the hand-offs. If you're open, I'll share how that would look in your environment." Point, proof, path.

Sales: Begin with the customer's tension, not your features. "You're paying for capacity you can't see. In two weeks, we can make the invisible visible, then cut it." Attention follows relief.

Ministry: Start by honoring the ache in the room. "Some of us barely made it here. You did—so let's breathe, and then listen for a line that will carry us through Wednesday." Your window becomes a shelter, then a summons.

Family: Respect sets the weight. "We both want quiet mornings. Here's a plan that gets lunches made without waking everyone." You're not performing; you're peacemaking.

♥ Daily practice plan (15 minutes)

Minute 1–3: breathe + posture + voice warm-up (hum on an "m," read two sentences slowly).

Minute 4–8: three random prompts; answer each using AAA-A + one structure (rotate PREP/PCS/PPF/SCQA).

~~~~~~~~~~~~~~ •••••••• ~~~~~~~~~~~~~

"Preparation, I have often said, is rightly two-thirds of any venture."

— Amelia Earhart

Minute 9–12: refine one answer into a micro-story with a sensory anchor.

Minute 13–15: bank what worked (one sentence + tags). Tomorrow, start with yesterday's bank.

A garden thrives by tending. So will your first fifteen seconds.

The single sentence you can memorize

If you only remember one line, make it this: ***"Anchor the moment, answer the question, advance with proof, ask for the next step."*** Say it under your breath before you speak. It is the compass that points any conversation north.

♥ Closing—own the window, serve the moment

You are not at the mercy of first impressions; you are the craftsman of them. When the window opens, do not rush to fill it with words. Fill it with presence, with a sentence that relieves confusion, with a gesture that signals respect, with a pace that lets truth land. The world is crowded with noise; your advantage is clarity in the first breath. Let your opening carry the quiet authority of someone who knows what matters and who is here to serve it.

You will still stumble, because all real speakers do. "What will change?" is what stumbles *mean*. Instead of proof you were never ready, they will be proof you are human—and prepared enough to steer anyway. That is the promise of the 15-Second Window: not perfection, but direction. Take it. Use it. And from the first syllable, lead

~~~~~~~~~~~~~ ●●●●●●● ~~~~~~~~~~~~~
"Fear thrives in the absence of structure."
— **Doctor Perspective™**

Chapter 3

Think Fast... Speak Smart

Look out for...

14) *The core challenge of rapid-fire thinking is balancing speed with clarity.*

15) *With enough rehearsal, the brain learns to categorize questions into familiar types.*

16) *Naming your dominant fear is the first step in loosening its grip.*

17) *Unless it is named and mastered, fear will always dominate the first 15 seconds.*

18) *That's what a great first response feels like—coiled, balanced, directed.*

19) *The pause is not hesitation—it is orchestration.*

20) *Theory is only as powerful as practice.*

21) *In communication, you are fighting a fire of another kind—fear, adrenaline, and uncertainty.*

♥ The Challenge of Rapid-Fire Thinking

In high-stakes situations—whether a job interview, a boardroom debate, or a live Q&A session—your ability to think fast under pressure makes the difference between influence and irrelevance. Rapid-fire thinking is not about blurting out the first idea that comes to mind but about disciplining your brain to access clarity on demand. Neuroscience shows that when adrenaline spikes, the brain's frontal lobes can become flooded, impairing reasoning. Seasoned communicators anticipate this and train themselves to treat adrenaline not as an enemy but as a cue to lock in.

The core challenge of rapid-fire thinking is balancing *speed with clarity*. If you speak too slowly, you lose the moment. If you speak too quickly, you risk incoherence. Success lies in cultivating reflexes that allow your mind to generate concise, relevant, and compelling answers in real time. These reflexes do not emerge overnight. They are trained, tested, and reinforced through deliberate practice.

Illustrative Example: The Courtroom Cross-Examination

Imagine a defense attorney cross-examining a witness. Every pause, every hesitation, could be interpreted as weakness or a crack in the case. The attorney must draw from a vast bank of knowledge while framing questions with speed, precision, and persuasive force. A misstep could confuse the jury or open the door to damaging counter-arguments. Here, the stakes are not simply about sounding articulate—they are about winning credibility when seconds matter.

The same pressure exists outside the courtroom. Politicians facing hostile media interviews, doctors briefing teams in emergencies, and executives on quarterly earnings calls all share the same reality: *hesitation erodes confidence, while clear speed builds it*. The challenge is not merely

◇ ♦ ◊ ♦ ◊— ♣— ♣—◊ ♦ ◊ ♦ ◊— ♣— ♣—◊ ♦ ◊ ♦ ◊

"Practice is nine tenths."

— **Ralph Waldo Emerson**

answering quickly but answering in a way that projects authority and steadiness.

♥ Neuroscience Behind the Challenge

When faced with rapid-fire demands, the brain's *amygdala* often triggers a fight-or-flight reaction. This can drown out the logical reasoning of the *prefrontal cortex*. Left unchecked, you end up rambling, stuttering, or drawing blanks. However, research on *neuroplasticity* shows that by repeatedly training under time constraints, you can rewire your neural pathways to respond calmly and sharply. Practicing with deliberate drills effectively conditions your brain to override panic and shift immediately into structured clarity.

One method often cited in psychology is *pattern recognition*. With enough rehearsal, the brain learns to categorize questions into familiar types. Instead of perceiving each new question as a unique crisis, the mind identifies patterns—challenge, clarification, objection, pivot—and applies prepared mental templates. This reduces processing time and allows faster, sharper answers.

Practical Drill

Take a random news article and give yourself only *30 seconds* to summarize it into three key points. Repeat this daily. The first few attempts will feel chaotic. But over time, your brain adapts: you learn to strip away clutter, prioritize essentials, and communicate crisply under pressure. This exercise mimics real-world situations where you don't have the luxury of meandering explanations. You must capture attention immediately.

Real-World Anecdote

During a televised debate, a candidate was asked an unexpected question about international trade. Instead of fumbling, she paused for a split-second, segmented her thought into three clear statements—impact on jobs, impact on national security, impact on future policy—and delivered them within sixty seconds. Analysts later noted that while her opponent gave a longer, more detailed response, it was her brevity and clarity that won audience approval. This demonstrates the paradox of rapid-fire thinking: ***less time can lead to more impact if structure is in place***.

The Cost of Failure

On the flip side, failing to master rapid-fire thinking can derail credibility. A manager fumbling through an answer in front of their team not only weakens the point but undermines authority. A sales professional who rambles through objections risks losing the sale. The brain's natural tendency under stress is to default to filler words— "uh," "you know," "like"—which signal uncertainty. Every wasted second dilutes impact.

Building Mental Reflexes

Think of rapid-fire thinking like a martial art. A martial artist doesn't wait to invent a move in the middle of a fight; they draw from trained reflexes honed through thousands of repetitions. Similarly, the skilled communicator does not invent clarity under pressure—they draw upon ***pre-trained clarity patterns***. With practice, these patterns become second nature. Your goal is to reduce the gap between question and structured answer from minutes to seconds.

♥ Fear 101 – The Hidden Barrier to Impromptu Clarity

Behind every hesitation, every blank mind, and every rambling answer lies one common enemy: fear. Neuroscience and psychology confirm what every Impromptu speaker feels—fear hijacks clarity. It narrows focus, speeds the heart, and clouds judgment. Unless it is named and mastered, fear will always dominate the first 15 seconds.

The Five Faces of Fear

Neuroscientist Dr. Theo Tsaousides identifies five distinct fears that surface in high-pressure moments:

Fear of Rejection – *"What if they don't like my answer?"* This fear leads to overcompensation, rambling to gain approval.

Fear of Failure – *"What if I blow this?"* It creates paralysis, where words refuse to come.

Fear of Judgment – *"They'll think I'm incompetent."* This fear produces safe, bland answers that fail to connect.

Fear of Embarrassment – *"I might look foolish."* Often causes defensive humor or awkward filler.

Fear of the Unknown – *"I don't even know where this is going."* Triggers panic, rushing, or avoidance.

Each fear is real. Each leaves fingerprints on your delivery. And each can be countered with awareness and practice.

Reflection Exercise

Pause and ask yourself:

Which of these five fears most often grips me when I speak without preparation?

What physical signs show up—sweaty palms, dry mouth, racing thoughts?

How have I responded in the past—by freezing, rambling, or joking it off?

Write your answers down. Naming your dominant fear is the first step in loosening its grip.

Why This Matters

Impromptu mastery is not the absence of fear but the ability to **speak through fear**. Just as athletes perform under pressure by training for the adrenaline surge, speakers can train for fear. By identifying its form, you prevent fear from dictating your first words. Instead, you take control of the moment.

——— ✦ ——— ✦ ——— ✧ ✧ ✧ ✧ ✧——— ✦ ——— ✦ ———

"Framework fluency is what makes you look not rehearsed,
but responsive."

— Doctor Perspective™

♥ The 3-Second Mental Triage Method

When confronted with a difficult question, the natural impulse is to rush into an answer. Yet the most effective communicators don't panic. Instead, they pause—just long enough to triage their thoughts. This is where the *3-second mental triage method* comes in. By taking three deliberate seconds before responding, you train yourself to override impulsive blurting and harness structured clarity.

The method mirrors what doctors and emergency professionals do when they must prioritize under pressure. In a trauma unit, a medic quickly sorts patients by urgency: who needs immediate surgery, who needs stabilization, and who can wait. This triage saves lives. In communication, the same principle saves credibility. You don't have unlimited time, but you do have a few precious seconds to decide whether to *reframe, redirect, or respond directly*.

Why 3 Seconds?

Cognitive research shows that the prefrontal cortex—the brain's center for reasoning—needs only a brief pause to suppress the amygdala-driven panic reflex. Three seconds is long enough to halt a rambling reaction but short enough to avoid awkward silence. It is a disciplined pause that communicates control. Instead of appearing hesitant, you appear thoughtful. Instead of blurting, you choose deliberately.

Application in Networking

Imagine you are at a networking event and someone asks: *"What's your biggest professional failure?"* Many people stumble here, either denying failure or rambling into excuses. By applying the 3-second triage, you silently count—*one, two, three*. In that pause, you decide:

Should you *reframe* by turning the question toward lessons learned?

Should you *redirect* to highlight resilience and current strengths?

Or should you *respond directly* with a concise story of recovery?

Because of the pause, you choose deliberately. You answer: *"My biggest failure was launching a project without testing it properly. The lesson? Today, I never skip validation. That failure now protects me from bigger mistakes."* The result: confidence and clarity. The silence between question and answer works in your favor, not against you.

Example from Media

In a live press conference, a politician was confronted with a hostile question: *"Are you lying to the public about this policy?"* An impulsive reaction could have spiraled into defensiveness. Instead, the politician paused for three seconds, reframed the question, and answered: *"What I owe the public is clarity. Let me explain the facts."* That pause and pivot shifted the tone from accusation to authority. Analysts noted afterward that those three seconds won credibility more effectively than a five-minute defense could have.

Neuroscience at Work

The pause activates your ***executive function***—your ability to weigh choices quickly. Neuroscientists call this the shift from **System 1 thinking** (fast, impulsive, emotional) to **System 2 thinking** (deliberate, logical, controlled). In rapid-fire exchanges, you cannot live in System 2 fully—it's too slow. But the 3-second pause is a bridge. It gives System 2 just enough room to shape System 1's instinctive output into structured clarity. This is how elite speakers appear both quick and composed.

Practical Drill

Practice the triage method in ordinary conversations. The next time someone asks you a routine question— *"How was your weekend?"*—apply a 3-second pause. Though the stakes are low, the training is high. Your brain learns to welcome silence rather than fear it. Over time, this micro-pause becomes second nature, and you deploy it automatically when the stakes rise.

You can also build this reflex by rehearsing ***controversial or awkward questions*** under timed drills. Record yourself answering, then

"No plan survives first contact with the enemy."
— Helmuth von Moltke

review whether the pause sharpened your response. Often, you'll notice that your words feel more intentional and less scattered.

Real-World Parallel

Think of a firefighter entering a burning building. He has seconds to decide whether to advance, retreat, or call for backup. Training ensures he does not panic but instead follows a triage sequence that has been drilled into muscle memory. In communication, you are fighting a fire of another kind—fear, adrenaline, and uncertainty. The triage pause is your oxygen mask, helping you breathe and respond with clarity instead of smoke-filled panic.

The Perception of Authority

The beauty of the triage method is not just in the content of your answer but in its perception. Audiences interpret pauses as signs of confidence. They think: *"She's not rattled. He's not defensive. They're in control."* In cultures that prize quick wit, this may seem counterintuitive, but the best rapid thinkers are not the fastest talkers—they are the fastest decision-makers. Pausing for three seconds is not losing time. It is buying time to win credibility.

Integration with Rapid-Fire Thinking

When paired with Section 1's emphasis on **mental reflexes**, the triage method becomes the gateway to structured speed. First, you train your brain with drills so that reflexive clarity is available. Then, in real-world use, you apply the pause to choose the best reflex. Together, they form a rhythm of rapid yet deliberate communication. The pause is not hesitation—it is orchestration.

♥ Filtering Noise, Finding the Gold

Every conversation is filled with noise. Some of it is verbal—irrelevant details, off-topic tangents, nervous filler words like *"um"* and *"you know"*. Some of it is emotional—anxiety, overthinking, or preoccupation with how you are being judged. And some of it is informational—the overwhelming

✳✳✳✳✳✳✳✳✳✳— ♣ — ♣ —✳✳✳✳✳✳✳✳✳✳

"Audiences perceive spontaneity as authenticity."

— **Doctor Perspective™**

flood of facts, statistics, and half-truths that obscure the central point. In the middle of this storm, the skilled communicator does not attempt to process everything. Instead, they filter the noise and uncover the gold.

Filtering noise is not about ignoring people or rushing past details. It is about *discernment*—the ability to separate what matters from what does not. A strong filter sharpens your focus and ensures that when you speak, your words are anchored to the essential truth of the moment.

The Cognitive Science of Filtering

Cognitive science confirms that human brains process an enormous amount of information every second—about *11 million bits unconsciously* but only *40 bits consciously*. That means 99.99% of incoming data never makes it to your awareness. Without a deliberate filter, your conscious mind becomes swamped by irrelevant signals. Skilled communicators deliberately guide those 40 conscious bits toward the golden nugget worth expressing.

This explains why some speakers sound scattered while others sound laser-focused. The difference is not intelligence but filtering. Those who filter well extract the three or four insights that matter most and discard the noise. In doing so, they appear calm, authoritative, and compelling.

Real-World Example: Newsroom Reporters

Newsroom reporters on deadline are masters of filtering. Faced with hundreds of pages of raw information—witness accounts, government reports, conflicting statistics—they cannot include everything. Their job is to extract the gold: the facts that define the story. A news anchor cannot ramble for twenty minutes. They must deliver a 90-second segment that captures both the essence and the urgency. That requires brutal discipline in separating the core from the clutter.

Impromptu speakers can learn from this. Your "deadline" is the moment the question ends and all eyes are on you. Your filter is the discipline that lets you ignore noise and deliver only the gold.

Practical Drill: The 60-Second Article

Here's a drill used by debate teams: take a dense article, perhaps an academic paper or a long editorial, and give yourself one minute to read it. Then, in the next minute, explain the three most important points aloud. At first, you may struggle. But over time, your brain adapts. You start scanning for signal words, identifying main arguments, and discarding fluff. Soon you can walk into any conversation, filter instantly, and frame the essentials.

Another version of this drill is called ***"Twitter Summarizing"***—boil an argument down to 280 characters or fewer. Though artificial, it trains you to distill ideas. Even if you expand later, your communication begins anchored to clarity.

Nature Parallel: The Hummingbird

The hummingbird, flapping its wings up to 80 times per second, appears frantic at first glance. Yet it is astonishingly precise. Amid the blur of motion, it hovers with perfect stillness over a single nectar source. Everything else—the wind, the noise, the competing flowers—is filtered out. It locks in on the one thing that sustains it.

Likewise, effective speakers hover over the nectar of their message. Amid the blur of adrenaline, questions, and distractions, they filter noise until only the gold remains. They may be moving fast outwardly, but inwardly, they are anchored by precision.

♥ The Cost of Poor Filtering

What happens when you fail to filter? You overtalk, overshare, and overexplain. You attempt to answer every angle, every nuance, and every possibility. Instead of sounding thorough, you sound scattered. Worse, your audience forgets everything except the impression of confusion.

One senior executive once summarized it this way: *"If you say ten things, I'll remember none. If you say three things, I'll remember all."* Filtering is not reduction for its own sake—it is reduction for impact.

The Discipline of Silence

Silence is one of the most underrated tools of filtering. By pausing mid-sentence, you allow your own brain to decide what comes next, and you allow the audience to digest what has already been said. A filtered communicator does not fear silence. Instead, they use it as punctuation—a way of highlighting the gold.

Integration with the Triage Pause

Filtering noise connects directly with the *3-second triage method* of Section 2. The triage buys you time. Filtering ensures you use that time wisely. The pause lets you sort. The filter lets you select. Together, they ensure that your answer is not only quick but also rich with substance.

♥ Real-World Example – Newsroom Reporters on Deadline

If you want a living masterclass in rapid-fire thinking, walk into a newsroom five minutes before a broadcast. Reporters are not sitting calmly at desks; they are sifting through chaos. Wire services are buzzing with updates, phones are ringing, editors are shouting changes, and new facts are streaming in by the second. Out of this storm, the reporter must craft a coherent story—fast, sharp, and accurate. That pressure cooker is the perfect model for Impromptu speaking.

A reporter doesn't have time for perfect phrasing. They have time only for *priority judgment*. They must decide: Which facts are relevant? Which quotes are usable? Which numbers are credible? And—most importantly—what angle will make the story clear and compelling for the audience? They cannot include everything. They must filter ruthlessly and deliver concisely.

※※※※※※※※※※— ♣ — ♣ —※※※※※※※※※※

"I have made this letter longer only because I had not the leisure to make it shorter."

— Blaise Pascal

Case Study: Covering Breaking News

During a natural disaster, a local reporter received conflicting reports: one official confirmed casualties, another denied them; eyewitnesses exaggerated numbers; social media spread misinformation. The reporter had twenty minutes before airtime. She chose three solid facts: the location, the scale of damage, and the government's immediate response. With those three points, she built a 90-second report. It wasn't exhaustive, but it was reliable, and it communicated the truth under deadline pressure.

This example mirrors Impromptu communication. You rarely have the luxury of endless explanation. The skill is in distilling chaos into clarity. The audience doesn't need everything—they need the essential.

The Power of Deadlines

Deadlines are not enemies; they are catalysts. In speaking, the moment a question ends is your deadline. Just as a reporter cannot delay the 6:00 p.m. broadcast, you cannot delay your answer. What reporters learn is that pressure, when embraced, creates discipline. Instead of rambling, they cut, sharpen, and aim. You must do the same. Think of every question as a breaking news deadline.

Practical Drill: The 60-Second Report

Borrow the newsroom method for training. Take any unfolding story—a sports event, a business headline, a personal anecdote—and give yourself 60 seconds to present it as if live on air. Set a timer. Your goal is not elegance but clarity. Identify the "who, what, when, where, why, how" and deliver them without fluff. Repeat until the habit of compressing into essentials becomes second nature.

Another variation: Have a friend throw random "breaking news" scenarios at you— "The school cafeteria has run out of food," "A major traffic jam blocks the highway," "A new product launch has gone wrong." With only one minute, build and deliver a coherent update. At first, you'll stumble. But with practice, your brain learns the newsroom discipline: decide fast, cut noise, hit clarity.

Lessons for Leaders

Executives, teachers, pastors, and parents all face "newsroom moments." An employee challenges them in a meeting. A student asks a hard question. A child asks for guidance on a sensitive topic. These are deadlines. The ability to filter and respond quickly is not a luxury—it is leadership in action. Leaders who ramble lose authority. Leaders who distill chaos into clarity inspire confidence.

Integration with Sections 1–3

This newsroom example ties directly to the earlier principles:

Rapid-fire thinking (Section 1) gives you reflexive speed.

The triage pause (Section 2) buys you just enough time to sort.

Filtering noise (Section 3) ensures only essentials make it through.

The newsroom model (Section 4) shows how those principles look in real life, under relentless deadlines.

This integration builds a holistic framework. Each principle is not a standalone trick; together they form a communication system. You train reflexes, apply the pause, filter for gold, and then package like a reporter on deadline.

♥ Nature Illustration – Hummingbird Precision

The hummingbird is one of nature's marvels. Its wings beat up to 80 times per second, creating a blur of motion that looks chaotic to the human eye. Yet within that chaos is astonishing control. The hummingbird can hover midair, reverse direction instantly, or land on a flower no wider than a dime. It does not waste energy flapping aimlessly; every movement is calibrated; every beat of its wings is purposeful.

~~~~~~~~~~~~~~ •••••••• ~~~~~~~~~~~~~

"Master the unscripted and you master the moment."

— Doctor Perspective™

This makes the hummingbird the perfect metaphor for rapid, high-stakes communication. When adrenaline surges and thoughts flutter, the untrained communicator resembles a sparrow—lots of flapping, little focus. But the skilled speaker channels energy like the hummingbird—rapid, precise, and always locked on the nectar of the message.

Why the Hummingbird?

Nature's design of the hummingbird is not accidental. Its muscles and reflexes are built for speed and accuracy. It processes visual information at a rate far faster than humans, enabling it to adjust instantly to shifting flowers, swirling winds, and competing distractions. The parallel for human communication is clear: ***speed without precision is wasted energy.*** The real skill lies in combining velocity with accuracy.

Application in Speaking

Picture a speaker in a live Q&A. The questions come fast. Audience members are restless. Time is short. An untrained speaker flaps wildly, trying to answer every detail, wasting words, and scattering attention. A skilled speaker, however, hovers. They focus on the nectar—the one essential point—and deliver it with clarity. Like the hummingbird, they may appear to move quickly, but every word is intentional.

For instance, in a corporate town hall, an executive was asked a complex question about restructuring. Rather than overwhelm with details, he distilled the answer into one clear message: *"Our priority is protecting jobs while ensuring long-term stability."* That single nectar point reassured employees more than a 20-minute explanation ever could.

Lessons from Nature

The hummingbird also teaches endurance. Despite burning energy at one of the highest rates in the animal kingdom, it thrives by feeding on concentrated nectar. In communication, your "nectar" is clarity. The clearer your message, the less energy you waste, and the more stamina you build for extended exchanges.

Another lesson is agility. Hummingbirds don't just fly forward—they can move backward, sideways, or hover. Similarly, skilled speakers adapt instantly. If a questioner challenges them, they pivot. If the audience shifts interest, they redirect. They don't get stuck in rigid scripts. They improvise without losing focus.

Practical Visualization

Before your next Impromptu speaking opportunity, visualize the hummingbird. Imagine the blur of wings and the laser focus on nectar. Let that image guide your response: move quickly, but land precisely. The act of visualization primes your brain, reminding you to choose precision over panic.

A practical drill: In practice sessions, allow someone to pepper you with rapid questions. Instead of answering each in long form, discipline yourself to give *one-sentence nectar answers*. Over time, this builds the reflex to hover over clarity rather than scatter over details.

Integration with Earlier Sections

The hummingbird metaphor unifies the entire chapter:

Section 1 taught you the challenge of rapid-fire thinking.

Section 2 introduced the triage pause.

Section 3 showed how to filter noise.

Section 4 gave the newsroom model.

Section 5 crowns the framework with a *nature image that makes the skill unforgettable.*

Every time you face pressure, the hummingbird reminds you: flap fast if you must, but never lose the nectar.

♥ Action Steps – Training Your Rapid-Fire Clarity

Theory is only as powerful as practice. The techniques of rapid-fire thinking—the triage pause, noise filtering, newsroom discipline, and hum-

◊♦◊♦◊— ♣— ♣—◊♦◊♦◊— ♣— ♣—◊♦◊♦◊

"Brevity is the soul of wit."

— **William Shakespeare**

mingbird precision—must be drilled until they become reflex. This final section gives you ***practical, repeatable steps*** that convert insight into skill.

1. Adopt the 3-Second Pause Daily

Every day, commit to pausing three seconds before answering at least five routine questions. These might be from colleagues, friends, or family. The goal is not to sound rehearsed but to train your brain to see silence as strength. Over weeks, this habit rewires your response pattern. Instead of panicking when put on the spot, you instinctively pause, triage, and respond with clarity.

2. Run the 60-Second Summarization Drill

Select a news article or opinion column. Give yourself one minute to read it and another minute to summarize aloud. Record yourself. Did you highlight essentials? Did you discard noise? Over time, this drill builds the habit of identifying signal words and structuring concise responses. Debate teams and corporate trainers use this exercise to sharpen thinking under deadlines.

3. Use the "Three Nuggets" Rule

No matter the complexity of the question, discipline yourself to deliver no more than three key points. Human memory thrives on triads: beginning, middle, end. Past, present, future. Problem, solution, benefit. By organizing answers into three nuggets, you increase recall and credibility. You can always expand later if invited, but the first impact must be sharp and memorable.

4. Visualize the Hummingbird

Before entering any high-pressure setting, close your eyes and imagine the hummingbird. See its blur of wings, feel its precision, and focus on its nectar. Let that visualization remind you to move quickly yet deliberately. This primes your subconscious to value accuracy over noise. Athletes visualize performance before competition; communicators can do the same.

5. Practice Newsroom Deadlines

With a friend or mentor, simulate "breaking news" questions. Give yourself 90 seconds to prepare and 60 seconds to deliver. Rotate through various topics: business, culture, leadership, personal values. The goal is not perfection but clarity under pressure. Over time, your mind learns that short deadlines are not threats—they are opportunities to show strength.

6. Build a Personal Question Bank

Collect tough questions you've faced—or fear facing. Write them on index cards. Randomly shuffle and answer them under timed conditions. By rehearsing responses to your greatest fears, you inoculate yourself against panic. What once caused dread now becomes routine.

7. Analyze Your Own Filler

Record three Impromptu answers and listen for filler words: *"um," "like," "you know."* Most people underestimate how often they use them. Awareness is the first step to elimination. Replace filler with purposeful silence. Each pause will strengthen the weight of your words.

8. Apply in Low-Stakes Environments

Don't wait for the boardroom or the big stage to practice. Use everyday moments. At dinner, summarize your day in three key points. In casual conversation, pause three seconds before answering. At the grocery store, explain your choice of product in one clear sentence. These small drills accumulate into reflexes that emerge when it matters most.

9. Embrace Adrenaline as Fuel

Instead of resisting nervous energy, reinterpret it. Adrenaline sharpens focus if you channel it. Tell yourself, *"This energy is my edge."* By reframing nerves as fuel, you transform potential panic into performance. This mental shift is the difference between flapping wildly and hovering like the hummingbird.

10. Reflect and Refine

After every Impromptu exchange, take two minutes to reflect. What worked? What faltered? What would you adjust? Reflection solidifies learning. Keep a journal of these moments. Over weeks and months, you will notice

patterns of growth and recurring pitfalls. This awareness accelerates mastery.

Call to Action

The challenge of rapid-fire thinking is universal. Everyone faces moments when eyes turn, questions land, and silence demands response. What separates leaders from the average is not innate brilliance but trained clarity. You now hold the framework: reflexes, pause, filtering, precision, action steps. The only task left is practice.

Commit today to the drills. Adopt the hummingbird mindset. Live like the newsroom under deadline. With every pause and every filtered response, you build the reflexes that turn panic into poise and hesitation into authority.

JOURNAL
Write it Down Before It Escapes!

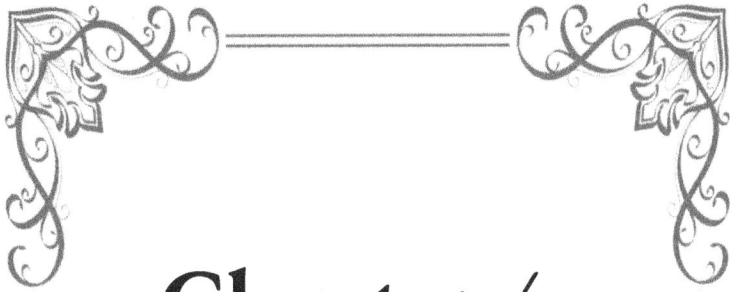

Chapter 4

Building Your Mental Toolbox

Look out for...

22) *Imagine stepping into a workshop. You would never reach for a hammer when a delicate screwdriver is required. Impromptu speaking works the same way.*

23) *Mental tools are not crutches. They don't weaken creativity; they support it. They don't trap you but free you. They are light-weight and easy to carry.*

24) *A jazz musician is not diminished by knowing scales— he is freed to improvise*

25) *"Spontaneity, paradoxically, is the fruit of preparation."*

26) *"Three stories, three quotations, three analogies—your Impromptu arsenal.*

♥ The Nature of Mental Tools

Imagine stepping into a workshop. On one wall hang saws, hammers, wrenches, drills—each designed for a precise purpose. You would never reach for a hammer when a delicate screwdriver is required. Impromptu speaking works the same way. When you are thrown a question with no preparation, you need a mental "toolbox" stocked with reliable instruments—frameworks, stories, quotations, devices, and models—that can be retrieved instantly.

A mental tool is any resource stored in your mind that helps you organize, clarify, or elevate your words under pressure. Unlike physical tools, these are weightless, portable, and infinitely adaptable. They save you from the paralysis of "what do I say?" by offering immediate pathways into structure and impact.

The key advantage of tools is speed. They allow you to bypass the mental bottleneck of invention and instead focus on selection. When the question comes—about leadership, education, ethics, or daily life—you do not start from zero. You reach into a mental drawer and pull out something pre-shaped, yet flexible.

Mental tools are not crutches. They don't weaken creativity; they support it. A jazz musician is not diminished by knowing scales—he is freed to improvise. In the same way, speakers with stocked toolboxes are freer to respond authentically and creatively because they know they can rely on proven structures.

This makes a toolbox essential for the 15-second dominator. Without it, you are gambling on inspiration. With it, you are positioned to shine under pressure.

♥ Preparation vs. Impromptu – The Hidden Paradox

Impromptu brilliance does not spring from thin air. It rests on the invis-

~~~~~~~~~~~~~~ •••••••• ~~~~~~~~~~~~~~
"Your voice is the most flexible instrument on earth. Fine-tune it and whatever you say will be music to the ears of your listeners."

— **Doctor Perspective™**

ible foundation of preparation. The pilot who makes a split-second adjustment in turbulence draws from thousands of training hours. The surgeon who chooses instantly in crisis relies on years of study and practice. The same is true of speakers: when you dazzle in the moment, it is because you've prepared long before the question was asked.

Spontaneity, paradoxically, is the fruit of preparation.

Your Toolbox in Practice

Start building a personal stockpile of material you can draw on at any time:

Three personal stories that can flex across many themes.

Three quotations or statistics you can trust and recall.

Three analogies from everyday life (nature, history, science, sports).

These nine tools, kept fresh and ready, form the backbone of your Impromptu arsenal. The more prepared your mind is with ready-made blocks, the freer you are to appear spontaneous.

♥ Stocking Your Toolbox with Frameworks

Frameworks are the skeleton that gives strength and shape to your words. They are not meant to trap you but to free you, giving you structure when time is short. If you try to speak without structure, your ideas spill out in fragments. If you lean on structure, your audience receives a clear and confident message—even in less than 15 seconds.

♥ PREP (Point–Reason–Example–Point)

This is the most dependable tool you can carry. Begin with your point. State a reason that supports it. Give an example that illustrates it. Then circle back and re-emphasize your point.

Question: "What makes a great leader?"

Point: "A great leader creates trust."

Reason: "Trust is the foundation on which influence stands."

Example: "Abraham Lincoln led a divided nation because people believed in his integrity."

Point again: "That's why trust is the core of leadership."

The PREP model turns scattered thoughts into a mini-speech with a beginning, middle, and end.

♥ Past–Present–Future

When a question deals with growth, change, or vision, this timeline framework is your ally.

Question: "How has communication evolved?"

Past: "It began as face-to-face storytelling around fires."

Present: "Today, we communicate instantly through screens and microphones."

Future: "Tomorrow, communication will be driven by virtual and AI interfaces, yet still depend on human connection."

The timeline gives natural movement and satisfies the listener's desire for orientation.

♥ Problem–Solution–Benefit

This is the persuasive framework. Define the problem. Suggest a solution. Highlight the benefit.

Question: "What should cities invest in first?"

Problem: "Many urban centers struggle with pollution."

Solution: "Investing in green public transportation cuts emissions."

Benefit: "Cleaner air improves health and raises quality of life."

Comparative Frameworks

Sometimes you need contrast. "On one hand... on the other hand... but overall..." is a simple pattern that shows balance.

Question: "Is technology good or bad for society?"

On one hand: "It connects us globally and speeds progress."

On the other: "It can isolate us and spread misinformation."

Overall: "It is a tool, and its impact depends on how we use it."

The Rule of One

When there's no time for length, reduce to one strong point. "If you remember nothing else, remember this." Audiences are more likely to recall one diamond than a handful of scattered pebbles.

By drilling these frameworks until they are second nature, you remove hesitation. Instead of asking, "What do I say?" you ask, "Which tool fits here?" That shift is the essence of mental readiness.

♥ The Power of Stories and Analogies

If frameworks are the skeleton of Impromptu speaking, stories and analogies are the lifeblood. They make ideas pulse with emotion and stick in memory. People rarely recall abstract points, but they remember the picture, the incident, the image that brought a principle to life.

Why Stories Work

Neuroscientists explain that when we hear stories, multiple regions of our brain activate—language centers, sensory centers, even parts tied to emotion. Facts touch the head; stories touch the heart. That combination makes a message unforgettable.

Anecdotes

The most versatile stories are short personal anecdotes. They don't need to be dramatic. A moment of failure, an embarrassing mistake, or a simple lesson from childhood can carry more impact than a grand historical tale.

Example: "I once froze when asked a question in front of my class. Later, I realized the silence didn't ruin me—it taught me the importance of preparation. That two-second failure gave me the two-decade habit of always carrying mental tools."

"Omit needless words."

— **William Strunk Jr.**

Analogies

Analogies compress truth into images. They let you explain something complex by connecting it to something familiar.

"Persistence is like water dripping on stone—it may be slow, but it reshapes mountains."

"Ideas are seeds. Left in your mind, they remain dormant. Shared, they grow."

"Speaking without structure is like building a house without a frame—it collapses under pressure."

With one comparison, you move your audience from confusion to clarity.

Everyday Moments as Gold

You don't need extraordinary experiences. Missing a bus, spilling coffee, planting flowers, repairing a tire—all can be transformed into illustrations. The secret is to develop the habit of noticing.

That is why keeping a ***story journal*** is one of the wisest practices for Impromptu speakers. Each evening, jot a few notes: "Saw a boy help his grandmother across the street. Felt inspired about service." Later, when a question arises on kindness, leadership, or responsibility, that tiny note becomes a powerful illustration.

The Power of Brevity

Impromptu stories must be trimmed. They need a beginning, turning point, and lesson—but in miniature. Learn to edit ruthlessly: one sentence for context, one sentence for action, one sentence for result.

In your toolbox, a dozen such anecdotes and half a dozen analogies can serve a lifetime of questions. They are renewable resources: the more you practice them, the sharper they become.

❋❋❋❋❋❋❋❋❋❋— ♣ — ♣ —❋❋❋❋❋❋❋❋❋❋

"A well-timed pause is the secret sauce of humor."

— Doctor Perspective™

♥ Quotations and Proverbs as Instant Authority

A short, well-placed quotation is like striking a match in a dark room—it lights the space instantly. Audiences instinctively lean in when they hear familiar wisdom or the voice of someone they respect. Quotations and proverbs give you borrowed credibility and rhythm in your delivery.

♥ The Weight of Quoted Words

A quote is powerful because it carries the authority of its source. When you invoke Lincoln, Mandela, Churchill, or Maya Angelou, you are not only speaking your thought—you are linking yourself with voices that have shaped history. That connection transfers weight to your words.

Guidelines for Using Quotations

Keep them short – A long quote drains time and focus. One sentence is often enough.

Attribute clearly – Name the source. "Einstein once said…" anchors the authority.

Use sparingly – If every answer is a string of quotations, you sound second-hand. Quotes should punctuate, not dominate.

Make them relevant – Tie the quotation directly into your point. Otherwise, it feels forced.

Examples

Inspirational: "Maya Angelou said, 'People will forget what you said, but they'll never forget how you made them feel.' That's why empathy matters in leadership."

Cultural: "An African proverb teaches, 'If you want to go fast, go alone.

~~~~~~~~~~~~~~ •••••••• ~~~~~~~~~~~~~
"Silence filled with calm is interpreted as thoughtfulness, not weakness."

— Doctor Perspective™

If you want to go far, go together.' That is the essence of teamwork."

Biblical/Spiritual: "Proverbs tells us, 'As iron sharpens iron, so one person sharpens another.' That is the principle behind accountability."

♥ Proverbs as Universal Connectors

Proverbs hold special power because they are cross-cultural. They have been tested by centuries and often carry poetic rhythm. Almost every culture has sayings about patience, wisdom, and courage. Using them builds a bridge of shared understanding.

Stocking Your Toolbox with Quotes

Select 10–20 quotations across common themes: courage, leadership, perseverance, kindness, vision, learning. Write them on cards or in a digital note. Practice weaving them into short responses until they flow naturally.

When your own words join forces with the authority of a respected voice, your impact doubles.

♥ Word Devices That Hook Audiences

Words are more than carriers of meaning—they are instruments of rhythm and music. The right device can make even a brief Impromptu answer sound polished, memorable, and deliberate. These are tools you can pull out instantly to add sparkle without stretching for time.

The Rule of Three

People remember things in threes. It feels complete, balanced, and satisfying.

"Courage, compassion, commitment."

"Think, speak, dominate."

A triad transforms a plain statement into something quotable.

Contrast

Opposites sharpen a point. Contrast frames your answer with tension and resolution.

"It's not about making a living; it's about making a life."

"We can be efficient without being effective, or we can be effective while being efficient."

Alliteration

Repetition of sounds adds rhythm. Used lightly, it makes your answer catchy.

"Discipline drives destiny."

"Purpose powers progress."

Rhetorical Questions

Questions that need no answer pull the audience into silent agreement.

"If not now, when? If not us, who?"

"What good is knowledge if it never becomes action?"

Parallelism

Repeating structure brings strength and cadence.

"We came, we saw, we spoke."

"I will stand for truth, I will speak with courage, I will serve with love."

Metaphorical Turns

Even a single metaphor gives lift.

"Ideas are seeds waiting for soil."

"Fear is a cage; courage is the key."

Strategic Pauses

Though not a word, silence is a device. A pause before the last phrase builds anticipation, letting your final words strike harder.

Mastering these devices does not mean cramming them into every sentence. It means having them at hand so that, when instinct calls for it, you can elevate your words from plain to powerful.

◇◆◇◆◇— ✣ — ✣ —◇◆◇◆◇— ✣ — ✣ —◇◆◇◆◇

"Clutter is the disease of American writing."

— **William Zinsser**

♥ Mental Models for Quick Reasoning

Frameworks give order, stories give life, quotations give authority, and word devices give polish. But sometimes what you need most in an Impromptu moment is a *lens*—a way to look at the question that instantly reveals an answer. That is what mental models provide.

Cause-and-Effect

This model asks two questions: *What caused this? What will it cause?*

Question: "Why do communities struggle with unity?"

Answer: "Division often begins with mistrust. That mistrust breeds isolation, which in turn weakens the whole fabric of society."

By following the chain, you can sound logical without preparation.

Pros-and-Cons

This model works when balance is expected.

Question: "Is technology making life better?"

Answer: "On the positive side, it connects us globally. On the negative, it sometimes isolates us personally. The challenge is finding balance."

It shows fairness and reflection.

Principle-Application

State a general truth, then apply it.

Question: "How should we handle power?"

Answer: "The principle is stewardship: power is meant to serve, not dominate. Applied to leaders, that means lifting others rather than controlling them."

Values Hierarchy

Every decision is a contest between values. Identify which comes first.

Question: "Should schools emphasize discipline or creativity?"

Answer: "Both are vital, but creativity without discipline flounders, while discipline without creativity stifles. Placing discipline first creates space for creativity to thrive."

Comparison by Metaphor

Sometimes the fastest reasoning is figurative.

Question: "What is success?"

Answer: "Success is a ladder. Some measure it by how high they climb, but true success is measured by how many others you bring up with you."

The Compass Test

Ask yourself, "Which direction should this point the audience—upward (inspiration), inward (reflection), outward (connection), or forward (action)?" Choose your answer accordingly.

These models don't lock you into a script—they unlock your thinking. Instead of freezing at the question, you let the lens give you the path.

♥ Emotional Levers – Connecting in Seconds

Facts inform, but emotions move. In a compressed moment of Impromptu speaking, emotion is often the fastest route to connection. By pulling the right lever, you shift your words from sounding like information to feeling like inspiration.

Humor

A touch of humor disarms tension and makes you relatable. The safest humor is self-directed.

"When I joined Toastmasters, my biggest fear was forgetting my speech. I solved it by forgetting it twice in the same meeting!"
Humor must never wound. Aim sideways or upward, never downward.

Empathy

Acknowledging shared experience builds instant rapport.

"We've all had mornings when nothing works—your alarm fails, your coffee spills, and your car won't start. Yet those days remind us we can still

"Your first defense is composure."
— **Doctor Perspective™**

smile through setbacks."

Empathy reassures listeners that you are one of them, not above them.

Inspiration

Sometimes the moment calls for vision.

"History is full of ordinary people who chose extraordinary courage. Why not us? Why not now?"
Inspiration lifts the listener's eyes to possibility.

Challenge

When appropriate, a direct challenge provokes reflection.

"What's stopping you from taking the first step today? Fear? Doubt? Or simply waiting for a perfect moment that may never come?"
A challenge stirs action where comfort keeps people still.

Blending Levers

You can weave them. Begin with empathy, lighten with humor, then turn to inspiration or challenge. This progression mirrors a natural emotional journey and feels authentic.

The secret is sincerity. A forced joke or hollow inspiration will collapse your credibility. But when the emotion rises naturally from who you are and what you believe, your 15 seconds can touch hearts as well as minds.

Practice: Stocking, Sharpening, and Selecting Tools

A toolbox is only useful if the tools are sharp, accessible, and chosen wisely. Many speakers collect tools but never test them. Others practice endlessly but never refine. To dominate in Impromptu speaking, you must **stock, sharpen, and select** with discipline.

Stocking

Begin by building your library of raw material.

Frameworks: PREP, Past–Present–Future, Problem–Solution–Benefit, and others.

Stories: Keep a journal of personal anecdotes and observations. Aim for a dozen polished micro-stories.

Quotations: Gather 10–20 versatile lines tied to themes like courage, learning, leadership, kindness.

Word Devices: Practice triads, contrasts, alliterations until they feel natural.

Mental Models: Identify your go-to lenses for analysis.

Stocking is about preparation. You cannot reach for what you never collected.

Sharpening

Tools dull without use. Sharpening comes through drills.

Daily PREP drill: Pick an object in the room and deliver a 15-second PREP speech.

Story trimming: Take a long story and reduce it to three crisp sentences.

Quotation test: Randomly select a theme and attach a relevant quotation from memory.

Device games: Speak for 60 seconds using only triads or contrasts.

Model practice: Apply cause-and-effect reasoning to a news headline.

These exercises turn theory into reflex.

Selecting

The master carpenter knows not just how to use tools, but which tool belongs to which task. The same applies here. When asked about leadership, you may choose PREP plus a story. When asked about technology, you may choose Past–Present–Future plus a quotation. The wrong tool—like humor in a funeral context—destroys credibility.

Selection grows with wisdom. With practice, your instincts sharpen, and your choices become almost automatic.

✳✳✳✳✳✳✳✳✳✳— ♣ — ♣ —✳✳✳✳✳✳✳✳✳✳

"No word was ever as effective as a rightly timed pause."

— Mark Twain

The speaker who builds, sharpens, and selects with care will never be caught empty-handed.

Real-World Example – The Airplane Conversation

Picture yourself on a flight. The person next to you, curious after some small talk, asks: *"What's your philosophy of leadership?"* You know the conversation will be cut short by the flight attendant in less than half a minute. You have a narrow window—your 15 seconds to leave an impression.

Without a toolbox, you scramble. Thoughts collide, your tongue trips, and you mutter something vague. The moment passes, and so does your chance to influence.

With a toolbox, the scene unfolds differently:

Framework: You reach instinctively for PREP.

Point: "Leadership is about trust."

Reason: "Without trust, people may obey out of fear, but they will never follow from the heart."

Example/Story: "I once had a coach who never raised his voice, yet we gave him our best because we trusted he believed in us."

Quotation: "As John Maxwell says, 'A leader is one who knows the way, goes the way, and shows the way.'"

Device: "Lead with head, heart, and hands."

Restatement: "That's why leadership always begins with trust."

The entire answer fits within 20 seconds. It sounds thought-out, polished, and personal. The stranger now sees you not just as a seatmate but as someone with insight worth remembering.

These small, everyday conversations are the proving ground for Impromptu speaking. If you can dominate in the aisle of an airplane, you can dominate on a stage, in a meeting, or in a boardroom.

♥ The Science Behind the Toolbox

Behind the art of Impromptu speaking lies science. Your brain under pressure does not behave the same as your brain at rest. Stress narrows attention, accelerates heartbeat, and can even cause temporary blanks in memory. A mental toolbox is not just a convenience—it is a neurological advantage.

Working Memory Limits

Psychologists tell us that working memory can hold only about seven chunks of information at once, often fewer when stress intrudes. That means when you are asked a question, your mind cannot juggle every idea at once. A framework, quotation, or analogy acts as a "chunk," compressing complexity into a single handle you can grasp.

Cognitive Offloading

Think of a toolbox as a form of ***cognitive offloading***. Instead of inventing from scratch, you retrieve pre-shaped structures. The moment you grab PREP, you have four steps already built. That frees your brain to focus on expression and authenticity instead of panicking over structure.

Retrieval Practice

Research shows that the act of recalling knowledge strengthens memory more than passive review. This is why daily drills work. By forcing your brain to retrieve a framework or quotation under mock pressure, you make it faster and more reliable in real conditions.

Emotional Resonance

Stories and analogies engage more brain regions than logic alone. Imaging studies show that narratives activate sensory and emotional areas, making the listener more engaged and more likely to remember. This explains why a short story often outlasts a long explanation in people's minds.

♥ The Role of Pauses

Neuroscience also supports the power of pauses. A brief silence gives the brain time to catch up and the audience time to absorb. What feels like a dan-

※※※※※※※※※※—♣—♣—※※※※※※※※※※
"Audiences are quick to judge. Influence their verdict"
— **Doctor Perspective™**

gerous gap to the speaker often feels like gravitas to the listener.

In short: the science proves what practice reveals. A well-stocked toolbox reduces load, increases fluency, and multiplies impact. It transforms chaos into clarity, panic into power.

♥ Cautions – The Wrong Use of Tools

Every tool can build, but misused it can also break. A well-stocked toolbox is powerful, but only if applied with wisdom. Misapplication can make you sound mechanical, irrelevant, or even insensitive.

Over-Tooling

Trying to use too many tools at once clutters your answer. Packing a framework, a story, a quote, a device, and a challenge into 15 seconds overwhelms the listener. Choose one or two that serve the moment best.

Mechanical Delivery

Frameworks are guides, not straitjackets. If you sound like you are checking boxes— "Point, Reason, Example, Point"—your delivery becomes robotic. Blend the structure with natural rhythm so that your audience hears a message, not a formula.

Irrelevant Stories

A good story at the wrong time is a distraction. If you are asked about resilience and you tell a story about your pet parrot, the disconnect breaks trust. Relevance is non-negotiable.

Over-Quoting

Quotations can enrich, but overuse makes you sound like an anthology. Audiences want your voice first. Let quotes support you, not replace you.

Forced Humor

Humor is fragile. If it feels strained or inappropriate, it backfires. A joke that falls flat is remembered longer than a point that landed well. Test your humor in safe settings before using it in high-stakes ones.

Ignoring Context

The right tool in the wrong context becomes the wrong tool. A playful story in a funeral tribute or a light joke in a crisis undermines credibility. Sensitivity to setting, audience, and timing is as important as the tool itself.

The wise speaker knows not only how to use tools, but when **not** to. Mastery lies in discernment.

Nature as Illustration – The Toolbox of a Bird

Nature often models what human effort must learn. Consider the bird building its nest. It does not depend on one material. It gathers twigs for structure, leaves for cover, feathers for softness, mud for cohesion, and sometimes even bits of string or cloth for strength. Each piece alone is insufficient, but together they create a shelter strong enough to survive storms and gentle enough to cradle life.

Your mental toolbox must resemble that nest. If all you collect are frameworks, your answers will sound rigid and skeletal. If all you rely on are stories, you may entertain but lack clarity. If you stock only quotations, you risk sounding borrowed. Variety ensures resilience.

The bird knows instinctively that diversity of material equals security. You must know consciously that diversity of tools equals readiness. Frameworks, stories, quotations, devices, models, and emotions—each plays a part. Together, they weave a nest of confidence that protects you from the winds of pressure and gives your audience a place to rest their trust.

Like the bird, gather continually. A twig today, a feather tomorrow, a string the next. Over time, your toolbox—your nest—will be more than enough for any storm.

♥ Call to Action – Build, Test, Refine

A toolbox is never finished. It is a living collection that must be built, tested, and refined. Without action, all of this remains theory. With action, it becomes transformation.

~~~~~~~~~~~~~~~ •••••••• ~~~~~~~~~~~~~~~

"Speak the speech, I pray you, as I pronounced it to you, trippingly on the tongue." — **William Shakespeare**

Build

Start gathering deliberately. Write down stories, even the small ones. Collect quotations that resonate with you. Note down analogies from daily life. Practice frameworks until they are instinct. The carpenter who never buys tools cannot build; the speaker who never gathers mental tools cannot dominate.

Test

Tools must be proven under pressure. Practice with friends, at an Impromptu Speech Club, in front of a mirror, or even on your commute. Put yourself under artificial time limits: "Answer this in 15 seconds." Testing reveals which tools are sharp and which are dull.

Refine

Not every tool fits your hand. Discard quotations that never land. Replace stories that drag. Adjust frameworks until they flow naturally in your voice. Refinement is the difference between a cluttered toolbox and a master's set of instruments.

By building, testing, and refining, you transform from a collector into a craftsman. When your moment comes, you will not grope in panic. You will reach with confidence, pull out the right tool, and deliver words that fit the moment.

The call is clear: start today. Every day you delay is another day you risk standing empty-handed when your 15-second window arrives.

Conclusion – From Panic to Power

The difference between the speaker who freezes and the one who flourishes is not intelligence—it is preparation. Panic comes when the mind faces a blank page. Power comes when the mind reaches into a toolbox already filled.

Frameworks give you shape. Stories and analogies give you life. Quotations and proverbs give you borrowed strength. Word devices give you polish. Mental models give you lenses. Emotional levers give you connection. Together, they transform you from a hesitant responder into a confident dominator.

Think of the bird's nest once more: twig by twig, it is woven into strength. So, your toolbox grows one framework, one story, one quotation at a time. Each addition is small, but over weeks and months it becomes a shelter against fear and a foundation for brilliance.

When the question comes without warning, you will not scramble. You will not shrink. You will breathe, reach inward, and know you are equipped. And in that moment—those 15 seconds that belong to you—you will turn silence into clarity, pressure into presence, panic into power.

That is the gift of a well-built mental toolbox. It is not just a set of tools— it is your confidence, your readiness, and your edge.

JOURNAL
Write it Down Before It Escapes!

◇◆◇◆◇—✤—✤—◇◆◇◆◇—✤—✤—◇◆◇◆◇
"One sentence is often enough. Two may be too many!"
— Doctor Perspective™

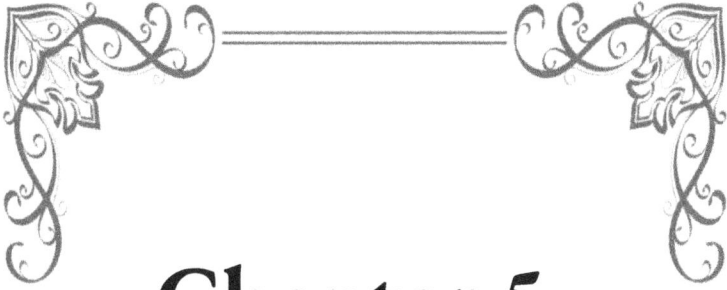

Chapter 5

The Power of the First Word

Look out for...

27) *The first word matters because it sets in motion the structure that frames everything else, and also because it seizes attention.*

28) *Avoiding weak openers is as critical as mastering strong ones.*

29) *Adopt the 3-second pause daily.*

30) *Energy matters as much as content.*

31) *Your mind learns that short deadlines are not threats— they are opportunities to show strength.*

32) *Collect tough questions you've faced—or fear facing... and conquer them.*

33) *The first word can be a wall—or it can be a welcome*

♥ Why the First Word Matters

The first word is more than a sound—it is the spark that ignites the entire response. Audiences form impressions in seconds, and often those impressions are hard to change. In Impromptu speaking, hesitation at the start can rob you of momentum, while a strong launch projects clarity and confidence.

Think of a sprinter. The race is not won in the first step, but a stumble at the start almost guarantees defeat. Likewise, the power of your first word sets your trajectory. A weak or wandering opening forces you to fight uphill. A crisp, confident first word propels you forward and gives your audience assurance that you know where you are going.

The first word also matters because it seizes attention. In a noisy room, in a distracted meeting, in a tense debate, the audience subconsciously asks: *"Is this worth listening to?"* A commanding first word—spoken with conviction—answers yes before the rest of your message even unfolds.

Finally, the first word matters because it anchors *you*. It steadies your nerves, reminds you that you are in control, and signals to your brain that the speech has begun. For many speakers, the greatest battle is not the middle or the end, but overcoming the inertia of silence. The first word breaks that silence, and with it, the fear.

Anatomy of a Two-Minute Speech

Even a brief Impromptu response can be structured like a miniature speech. In contests, evaluators often judge based on whether the speaker demonstrated an opening, body, and conclusion. Think of it as the anatomy of a two-minute speech: the first 15 seconds capture attention, the middle 90 seconds develops the thought, and the final 15 seconds deliver a crisp conclusion.

This is why the *first word* matters—it sets in motion the structure that frames everything else.

———— ✦ ———— ✦ ———— ✦ ———— ✦ ———— ✦ ————

"Suit the action to the word, the word to the action."

— William Shakespeare

Case Study

One club speaker began with, "Uh, that's a good question, let me think..." The hesitation drained the room's energy. Another began the same question with, "If you want to know my greatest teacher, it wasn't a person— it was failure." The bold first line captured every ear. Both had only two minutes, but the difference was decided in the first ten seconds.

♥ Psychological Impact on the Speaker

The first word does more than open the speech—it stabilizes the speaker. Before speaking, nerves may tighten the chest, dry the mouth, and cloud the mind. The silence feels heavy, and hesitation feeds anxiety. But once the first word leaves your lips, the burden shifts. You are no longer preparing—you are performing.

That first word acts like a key turning in a lock. It signals to your brain, *"I have started."* Adrenaline begins to channel into focus rather than fear. Muscle memory takes over, and the frameworks, stories, and tools you've rehearsed start to flow.

Psychologically, the first word also creates ownership. Until you speak, the stage feels hostile, the audience feels distant, and the question feels threatening. The instant you begin, all of those elements become yours—the stage is your space, the audience is your partner, the question is your canvas.

For the Impromptu speaker, this shift is critical. Without it, anxiety multiplies. With it, confidence compounds. That is why rehearsing not just answers but *openings* are essential. When you know how to start, you train your mind to move from silence to strength in a single breath.

♥ Psychological Impact on the Audience

Audiences are quick to judge. Long before your reasoning unfolds, they evaluate your confidence, clarity, and credibility. The very first word you speak tells them what to expect.

A hesitant start— "uh... well... maybe..."—signals uncertainty. Even if you recover, the audience may already have decided that you are unprepared. Conversely, a firm, clear opening word— "Leadership," "Absolutely," "Yes," or "Imagine"—immediately conveys control. It primes listeners to trust that you have something worth hearing.

The first word also sets the emotional tone. A bright, energetic "Yes!" prepares them for enthusiasm. A calm "Consider..." prepares them for reflection. A solemn "Friends..." invites intimacy. In less than a second, your audience's mood begins to mirror the mood of your opening.

Finally, the first word anchors attention. In a distracted room, many people tune in and out. A commanding start breaks through that fog and makes them turn their focus toward you. Like the crack of a starter's pistol, it signals that something has begun—something they should not miss.

In Impromptu speaking, you rarely have time to win attention gradually. The first word is your chance to seize it at once.

♥ Techniques for Launching Strong

If the first word carries such power, then mastering how to launch becomes essential. These techniques ensure that your opening word is not only heard but felt.

1. Use a Strong Anchor Word

Begin with a clear, decisive word that frames the topic.

"Courage."

"Leadership."

"Opportunity."

A single, commanding word steadies you and signals direction.

2. Begin with a Declaration

Start with confidence.

"Yes, technology has changed everything."

"An evasive or defensive answer erodes credibility."

— **Doctor Perspective™**

"No achievement is greater than learning to rise after failure."
A declarative launch projects certainty.

3. Ask a Provocative Question

Questions seize curiosity.

"What would you attempt if you knew you could not fail?"

"When was the last time you truly listened to someone?"
Questions invite the audience into dialogue rather than monologue.

4. Paint a Quick Picture

Visual openings grab imagination.

"Imagine standing at the base of a mountain with only one path upward."

"Picture a child seeing the ocean for the very first time."
A vivid image places listeners in the scene instantly.

5. Echo the Question – Don't Repeat it

If you need a second to gather your thoughts, restating the question is a subtle launch.

Question: "What does success mean to you?"

Answer: "Success, to me, means impact more than income."
This buys you time while still sounding intentional. Repeating the question is a not-so-subtle give-away that you may be stalling for time while you think. More than likely, this is so, but you do not want anyone else to know.

6. Harness Pauses

A silent breath before the first word builds anticipation. Audiences lean in, expecting power to follow.

With these techniques at hand, you no longer face the terror of beginning. You own the moment from the very first sound.

♥ Avoiding Weak Openers

Just as strong beginnings inspire confidence, weak openings instantly drain it. Many speakers sabotage themselves in the very first breath by falling into these traps:

1. Fillers

Starting with "uh," "well," "like," or "you know" tells the audience that you are scrambling. It signals disorganization before your message even begins.

2. Apologies

Opening with "I'm not really prepared..." or "This might not be very good..." undercuts your credibility. The audience will believe you. Never apologize for being caught off guard—own the moment.

3. Wandering Starts

Sentences that meander without direction— "You know, there are a lot of ways to look at this, and maybe we can consider..."—lose listeners before you land your point.

4. Repetition Without Purpose

Simply repeating the question word for word can sound like stalling unless it is followed immediately by insight. Echo, if necessary, but add value at once.

5. Over-Formality

Beginning with stiff formality ("Ladies and gentlemen, I stand before you today...") feels unnatural in Impromptu settings. It wastes precious seconds and distances you from the audience.

6. Monotone Delivery

Even the right word fails if delivered flatly. Energy matters as much as content. A dull "Yes" does not inspire. A confident, lifted "Yes" does.

Avoiding weak openers is as critical as mastering strong ones. The first

※※※※※※※※※※— ✚ — ✚ —※※※※※※※※※※

"Give every man thy ear, but few thy voice."

— William Shakespeare

impression is too valuable to waste on hesitation, apology, or filler.

♥ Case Studies of First Word Domination

Examples from real-world situations show how the first word can tilt the entire encounter toward success.

The Boardroom Pitch

A young manager was unexpectedly asked in a meeting: *"Why should we fund your project?"* Instead of fumbling, she looked directly at the decision-maker and began with one word: ***"Results."*** She then followed with PREP: "Results are what this project guarantees. Last quarter we cut costs by 15%. This quarter we'll double that. That's why the funding is justified." The single, strong opening word set the tone of authority.

The Classroom Challenge

A teacher once asked a student in debate club, *"What's the greatest threat to democracy?"* The student launched immediately with ***"Apathy."*** That single word framed the entire argument. Every sentence that followed supported it. The clarity of the first word became the clarity of the speech.

The Interview Seat

In a job interview, the candidate was asked: *"What motivates you?"* Instead of hesitating, she leaned forward and said, ***"Growth."*** Then she expanded: "Growth of myself, growth of my team, growth of the company." The interviewer later admitted that the confidence of that one-word opening secured the position.

The Contest Stage

During a Table Topics contest, the speaker drew the question: *"What would you change about the world?"* He smiled, paused, and declared, ***"Hope."*** Then he built a short speech around rekindling hope in individuals, families, and nations. The room erupted in applause—not because the answer was complex, but because the first word struck the heart.

These cases prove that the very first word can anchor the entire response. It defines your focus, projects confidence, and leaves a memorable impression long after the rest of your words fade.

♥ Practical Drills for First-Word Power

Strength in the first word does not come by accident—it comes by practice. The more you rehearse strong starts, the more natural they become under pressure.

One-Word Launch Drill

Pick a random theme—leadership, love, technology, fear. Force yourself to answer with a single, commanding first word: *"Integrity." "Compassion." "Innovation."* Build the rest of your response from that anchor.

Echo and Add Drill

Practice repeating the question briefly, then adding a decisive first word.

Question: "What is success?"

Answer: "Success? **Contribution.**" Then expand.

This keeps you from stalling while buying a second of thinking time.

Speed Round Drill

With a partner or timer, set 30 seconds for rapid-fire questions. Your only goal: start immediately with strength. Don't worry about the whole speech—train the reflex of confident beginnings.

Pause and Launch Drill

Practice taking a deliberate one-second pause before your first word. This settles nerves and signals control. After the pause, release a strong, clear word. The silence before the sound adds power.

Mirror and Record Drill Practice openings in front of a mirror or camera. Notice your face, eyes, and tone. Did your first word come across hesitant or commanding? Refinement comes from review.

Mastering first words is like a pianist practicing scales—it feels repetitive, but it builds instinct. When the real performance comes, your fingers—or in this case, your voice—will know exactly where to begin.

Conclusion – The First Word as the Seed of Success

The journey of an Impromptu response begins not with the middle or the end, but with the very first word. It is the seed from which everything else grows. A weak seed produces hesitation, doubt, and loss of trust. A strong seed produces clarity, confidence, and connection.

For the speaker, the first word shifts psychology from anxiety to action. For the audience, it sets the tone and signals whether your message is worth listening to. For both, it creates momentum that carries through the rest of your answer.

When you choose that first word with intention—whether it is a bold declaration, a vivid image, or a thought-provoking question—you anchor yourself and your audience in the same moment. From there, every sentence flows with greater force.

Practice will make this instinctive. Rehearse strong starts until your mind, even under pressure, instinctively rejects filler and apology, reaching instead for conviction. Over time, you will no longer fear beginnings. You will welcome them.

The first word is small, but it is decisive. It is the strike of the match, the starter's pistol, the first step onto the stage. When spoken with purpose, it does more than open a speech—it opens the door to domination.

~~~~~~~~~~~~~~ ●●●●●●●● ~~~~~~~~~~~~~~
"Energy matters... not just content."
— **Doctor Perspective™**

JOURNAL
Write it Down Before It Escapes!

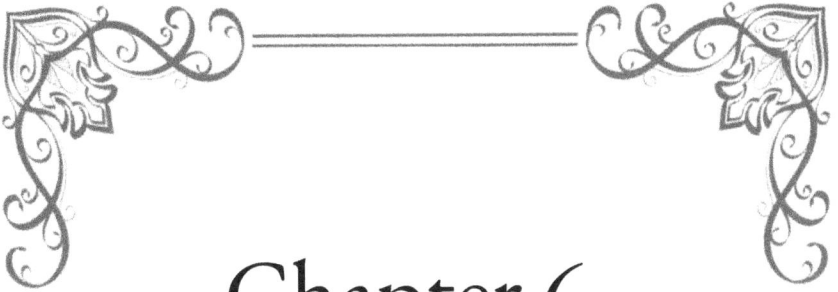

Chapter 6

The PREP and Beyond: Frameworks for Order Under Pressure

Look out for...

34) *Fear thrives in the absence of structure*
35) *Frameworks must respect the setting.*
36) *Frameworks should never draw attention to themselves.*
37) *Frameworks only serve you if they become second nature.*
38) *The most common mistake is making the framework too obvious.*
39) *PREP is designed for one Point, one Reason, one Example, one restatement.*
40) *Framework fluency is what makes you look not rehearsed, but responsive.*

♥ PREP as the Core Framework

If there is one framework that every Impromptu speaker must master, it is PREP—***Point, Reason, Example, Point.*** It is the simplest, most versatile, and most dependable structure in the entire toolbox. For more than half a century, PREP has been taught in debate clubs, Impromptu Speech Club meetings, classrooms, and boardrooms because it delivers order in the midst of pressure.

The genius of PREP lies in its clarity. In four steps, you give your audience a roadmap: state your answer, explain why it matters, ground it with a real or imagined illustration, and drive it home again. Each step is distinct, but together they create flow. Listeners know exactly where you are taking them, and you never appear lost.

Consider the question: *"What is the greatest quality of leadership?"*

Point: "The greatest quality of leadership is trust."

Reason: "Without trust, no one will follow willingly—obedience may come through fear, but loyalty never does."

Example: "Think of Nelson Mandela. After decades in prison, he emerged without bitterness, and because people trusted his integrity, he was able to unify a fractured nation."

Point again: "That's why leadership always rises or falls on trust."

Notice how PREP builds miniature completeness: beginning, middle, end. Even in 20 seconds, it feels like a speech rather than a reaction.

Another advantage is memory. PREP's four steps are easy to recall under pressure. When your mind freezes, remembering "Point, Reason, Example, Point" gives you a lifeline. The framework pulls you forward when nerves hold you back.

But PREP is more than safety—it is strength. It works across nearly every context: answering a contest Table Topic, responding to a tough interview

~~~~~~~~~~~~~~ •••••••• ~~~~~~~~~~~~~~
"A soft answer turns away wrath."

— **Proverbs 15:1**

question, or sharing an opinion at a board meeting.

Wherever clarity is needed fast, PREP delivers.

The secret is not just knowing PREP, but practicing it until it feels like instinct. When you can glance at any object—a pen, a chair, a tree—and instantly deliver a PREP mini-speech, you know you have internalized it. At that point, PREP stops being a formula and becomes second nature, the steady heartbeat of your Impromptu skill.

♥ Frameworks as Antidotes to Fear

Fear thrives in the absence of structure. The reason so many speakers freeze, ramble, or stall under pressure is not lack of intelligence, but lack of a reliable framework. PREP—Point, Reason, Example, Point—functions as an antidote to fear. It quiets the mental chaos by offering a ready-made pathway forward.

Imagine being asked a question about leadership. Without a framework, the mind races: *Where do I begin? How much detail do I give?* With PREP, you instantly know the path: state your point, give your reason, tell one clear example, and close by reinforcing the point. Order replaces panic.

Practical Exercise

Take a fear-inducing question like, *"Why should anyone follow you?"* Answer it once without a framework, noticing the stress or confusion it creates. Then answer again using PREP. You'll discover how much calmer, clearer, and more confident you feel when structure is on your side.

♥ Expanding Beyond PREP

While PREP is the bedrock, relying on it alone is like trying to build an entire house with only a hammer. You can drive nails, but you cannot cut wood, tighten bolts, or finish details. To dominate Impromptu speaking, you must broaden your framework inventory. Each alternative structure offers a unique rhythm and purpose.

Past–Present–Future

This framework provides natural movement through time. It works especially well for questions about growth, change, or vision.

Question: "How has communication evolved?"

Past: "For centuries, communication meant waiting weeks for letters carried by horseback."

Present: "Today, a text message travels the globe in a second."

Future: "Tomorrow, we may converse through virtual reality so realistic it will feel like teleportation."

Audiences love this structure because it orients them in time—it is easy to follow and feels complete.

Problem–Solution–Benefit

Ideal for persuasive settings, this framework makes you sound like a problem-solver.

Question: "What's one thing our community should focus on?"

Problem: "Many neighbors live side by side but rarely speak."

Solution: "Organizing monthly gatherings could rebuild those bonds."

Benefit: "A stronger sense of connection would make the community safer and happier."

This approach appeals to logic and emotion at once.

Comparative Contrast

When nuance is needed, contrasting two sides creates balance.

Question: "Is social media more helpful or harmful?"

Contrast: "On one hand, it connects families across oceans. On the other, it fuels misinformation. The truth lies in how responsibly we use it."

This structure shows you can weigh perspectives rather than rushing to extremes.

STAR (Situation–Task–Action–Result)

Perfect for personal or professional storytelling, STAR packages experiences cleanly.

Question: "Tell us about a time you overcame difficulty."

Situation: "In college, I was failing a crucial course."

Task: "I needed to raise my grade to graduate."

Action: "I formed a study group and committed to daily review."

Result: "I passed with one of the highest marks in the class."

In interviews or leadership moments, STAR shines.

Quote–Interpret–Apply

Sometimes the most effective answer begins with borrowed wisdom.

Question: "Why does perseverance matter?"

Quote: "Churchill once said, 'Never, never, never give up.'"

Interpret: "He understood that persistence often outlasts talent."

Apply: "For us today, perseverance means refusing to quit when obstacles mount."

This blends external authority with personal insight.

Rule of One

At times brevity is king. Landing one strong word or line can be more powerful than an entire framework.

Question: "What defines success?"

Answer: "Service."

That single word, delivered with confidence, can echo longer than a paragraph.

Expanding beyond PREP gives you flexibility. Instead of squeezing every

※※※※※※※※※※— ♣ — ♣ —※※※※※※※※※※※

"The question is your foundation."

— Doctor Perspective™

question into the same mold, you can match the moment with the right structure. This variety not only sharpens your delivery but keeps your audience engaged.

♥ **Comparative Strengths of Frameworks**

Each framework is a tool with its own unique strength. The more you understand what each does best, the more confidently you can match framework to moment.

PREP – The Universal Default

Strength: Works almost everywhere. Clear, logical, fast.

Best for: General questions, contests, quick answers where clarity is key.

Weakness: Can sound formulaic if overused without variety.

Past–Present–Future – The Visionary Lens

Strength: Shows progression and foresight.

Best for: Questions about growth, change, or predictions.

Weakness: Risks cliché if the "future" section is vague ("technology will change everything").

Problem–Solution–Benefit – The Persuasive Driver

Strength: Positions you as a solver, not just a thinker.

Best for: Business, leadership, social issues, or anytime action is needed.

Weakness: Falls flat if the "problem" is weak or the "solution" feels unrealistic.

Comparative Contrast – The Balance Keeper

Strength: Shows fairness and critical thinking.

Best for: Controversial or nuanced topics with two strong sides.

Weakness: If not resolved decisively, you risk sounding indecisive.

STAR – The Story Framework

Strength: Polishes personal or professional experiences.

Best for: Job interviews, leadership settings, or any "tell us about a time…" question.

Weakness: Longer—requires discipline to keep concise.

Quote–Interpret–Apply – The Authority Boost

Strength: Adds external weight and memorability.

Best for: Moral, motivational, or philosophical questions.

Weakness: Can feel forced if the quote is obscure or irrelevant.

Rule of One – The Impact Punch

Strength: Delivers unforgettable simplicity.

Best for: High-stakes openings, interviews, or moments when brevity has power.

Weakness: Too light when depth is expected.

The true master is not the one who knows one framework deeply, but the one who knows several well enough to choose the perfect fit in real time. Framework fluency is what makes you look not rehearsed, but responsive.

Pitfalls of Framework Use

Frameworks bring order, but when misused they can work against you. Many promising responses collapse because the speaker mishandled the very tool meant to help. Knowing the pitfalls ensures you avoid mechanical delivery and keep your answers authentic.

Sounding Formulaic

The most common mistake is making the framework too obvious. If your answer feels like a checklist— "First, here's my point… second, here's my reason…"—the audience hears the skeleton instead of the story. A framework should be invisible scaffolding, not a cage.

Overloading Each Step

Another danger is stuffing too much into every part. PREP is designed

◇ ◆ ◇ ◆ ◇— ✦ — ✦ —◇ ◆ ◇ ◆ ◇— ✦ — ✦ —◇ ◆ ◇ ◆ ◇

"Let every person be quick to hear, slow to speak, slow to anger."

— James 1:19

for one Point, one Reason, one Example, one restatement. Some speakers cram in three or four reasons and multiple examples. The result is clutter, not clarity. Less is more.

Choosing the Wrong Fit

Not every framework fits every question. Using STAR for an abstract question like "What is truth?" feels unnatural. Using Problem–Solution–Benefit for "Tell me about yourself" feels awkward. Forcing the wrong frame makes you sound mismatched and unprepared.

♥ Overreliance on One Model

When every answer sounds like PREP, audiences tune out. Variety keeps listeners engaged. Mix PREP with Past–Present–Future, Contrast, or STAR. Mastery means flexibility, not repetition.

Ignoring Context

A persuasive Problem–Solution–Benefit answer may shine in a debate but feel out of place in a casual dinner chat. A light "Rule of One" answer may inspire at a panel but fall flat in a high-stakes interview. Frameworks must respect the setting.

Neglecting Natural Delivery

A technically correct answer can still fail if delivered stiffly. Frameworks are meant to free your energy for voice, tone, and connection. If you sound robotic, you have missed their purpose.

Frameworks should never draw attention to themselves. Their role is to support *you*—to let your ideas shine with clarity, flow, and confidence. Use them wisely, and they become invisible allies.

Practice Routines for Framework Fluency

Frameworks only serve you if they become second nature.

In the heat of an Impromptu moment, you don't have time to recall a chart—you need instinct.

The only way to achieve that instinct is disciplined, varied practice until frameworks slip into your responses automatically.

Daily Object Drill

Pick an object near you—a glass, a book, a pen. Deliver a 30-second response using PREP, then repeat with a different framework. Example with a *book*:

PREP: "A book is a treasure. It teaches lessons. I remember reading one that changed my life. That's why books are priceless."

Past–Present–Future: "Books began as clay tablets. Today, they are digital downloads. In the future, books may be holograms."
This drill builds speed and adaptability.

Headline Framework Drill

Scan a news site or social feed. Take one headline and answer it using Problem–Solution–Benefit, then another using Comparative Contrast. For instance, a headline on climate change can quickly become:

Problem: rising temperatures.

Solution: renewable energy.

Benefit: a livable planet for the next generation.

STAR Story Rehearsal

Keep a list of personal stories—small wins, failures, turning points. Practice telling them in STAR form (Situation, Task, Action, Result) in under 60 seconds. When asked a personal question, your story is already packaged.

Framework Roulette

Write down different frameworks on slips of paper. Pull one at random before answering a question. This prevents over-reliance on PREP and forces mental flexibility.

"After you know what you want to say, the only task left is practice."
— Doctor Perspective™

Partner Toss

With a friend, trade quick questions. The rule: each must be answered in a *different* framework than the one just used. This develops fluency and prevents monotony.

Time Pressure Practice

Set a timer for 15 seconds. Deliver a complete framework response before it buzzes. This sharpens brevity without losing coherence.

Like musicians practicing scales or athletes running drills, speakers must treat frameworks as daily exercises. Over time, the effort dissolves into instinct. When the real question comes, you won't think *"Which framework?"*—you'll simply speak with order and confidence.

"Only the prepared speaker deserves to be confident."
— Dale Carnegie

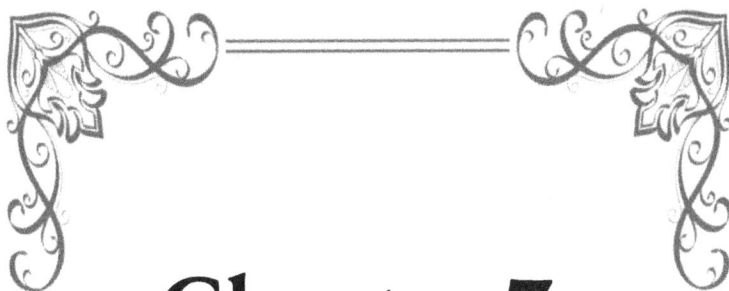

Chapter 7

Humor Without Risk: Wit That Wins, Not Wounds

Look out for...

41) *In the unpredictable world of Impromptu speaking, a laugh does more than lighten the mood—it establishes control.*

42) *Logic may earn agreement, but emotion creates memory.*

43) *Every Impromptu moment feels like a sprint against time. Humor slows the clock.*

44) *Humor expands your influence only when it protects dignity.*

45) *Wit is not memorized comedy—it is quick perception shaped into playful response.*

46) *Clean beats clever, and kind beats cutting—especially when a room is tense.*

Humor in Question Styles

Not every question is neutral. Some are designed to unsettle. Yet even the most challenging question styles can be turned into moments of levity. Two common patterns invite humor if handled wisely:

Absurd Questions – These are intentionally exaggerated or unrealistic. A speaker once faced, *"If you could be any fruit, which would you be?"* Rather than stumbling, she replied, *"I'd be a pineapple—tough on the outside, sweet on the inside, and with a crown on top."* The room laughed, and she turned nonsense into charm.

Truncated Questions – Sometimes a question is so short or vague it feels like a trap. A member was asked simply, *"Failure?"* He paused, smiled, and said, *"Failure is the tuition we pay for success."* The economy of words carried wisdom and humor together.

Handled carefully, these moments disarm tension, keep the mood light, and show the audience you can think and smile on your feet.

These quick examples show that humor is not an accident—it is a skill. By noticing the shape of the question and choosing wit that uplifts rather than wounds, you transform a trap into triumph. But humor is more than clever comebacks. To understand why it works so powerfully in Impromptu speaking, we need to look deeper at what humor does in the mind and in the moment.

Why Humor Works in Impromptu Speaking

Humor is one of the fastest bridges between a speaker and an audience. In the unpredictable world of Impromptu speaking, a laugh does more than lighten the mood—it establishes control. When people see you spark humor without preparation, they read it as confidence. That impression creates what psychologists call a "halo effect": if you can be funny under pressure, you must be capable in everything else you say. Humor becomes a credibility accelerator.

~~~~~~~~~~~~~~ ●●●●●●●● ~~~~~~~~~~~~~~

*"**Real humility** requires having value to offer, and effectively delivering it with clarity and sincerity*
— Doctor Perspective™

♥ The Psychology Behind Laughter

Laughter is chemistry as well as emotion. It releases endorphins, lowers stress, and strengthens social bonds. Studies in group dynamics show that people who laugh together trust each other more quickly. In a contest, that trust tilts judges in your favor. In a boardroom, it makes your ideas more palatable. In a classroom, it holds attention when focus might otherwise drift. Humor is not ornamental—it is neurological glue that binds speaker and listener.

♥ Humor as a Time Buffer

Every Impromptu moment feels like a sprint against time. Humor slows the clock. A playful line buys a few seconds of laughter, and in those seconds your mind regroups. Instead of filling silence with panic, you use humor as a pressure valve. A speaker in an Impromptu Speech Club delivery may slip in a humorous aside before launching into a story. A CEO fielding a tough question might chuckle at the wording before delivering a clear plan. In both cases, humor isn't stalling—it's tempo control, giving the speaker space to breathe and the audience a chance to lean in.

♥ Humor Creates Memorability

Logic may earn agreement, but emotion creates memory. A well-placed laugh becomes a mental bookmark. If two speakers deliver equal content, the one who made the audience chuckle is the one they recall afterward. Humor highlights your point like a yellow marker across the page. The message is not "this was funny," but "this mattered enough to remember."

♥ Humor as Humanity

Audiences forgive mistakes when they like the speaker. Humor accelerates likability because it shows humility and relatability. A quick quip— "Even my chair is nervous about this question"—turns nerves into warmth.

⁜⁜⁜⁜⁜⁜⁜⁜⁜— ♣ — ♣ —⁜⁜⁜⁜⁜⁜⁜⁜⁜
"A well-timed pause is the secret sauce of humor."
— Doctor Perspective™

Listeners think, *"They're human, like me."* That moment of recognition makes forgiveness natural if you stumble later.

♥ Humor as Strategy

Impromptu humor is not stand-up comedy. It is observation with a twist, exaggeration with restraint, or wordplay without cruelty. The rule is simple: keep it clean, kind, and often self-directed. Humor should be seasoning, not the meal—just enough to enhance, never so much that it overwhelms.

Used wisely, humor reduces tension, buys time, boosts recall, humanizes you, and sharpens impact. That is why, in Impromptu speaking, humor is not a luxury—it is a strategic necessity.

♥ The Boundaries of Safe Humor

Humor expands your influence only when it protects dignity. In Impromptu settings you can't beta-test a line, so you need guardrails that work everywhere. Think of boundaries as the frame that lets your wit shine without collateral damage. If a line risks harm, skip it. The audience will not miss what you wisely didn't say.

Never Punch Down

Do not aim humor at people with less power, less voice, or who cannot answer back. Audiences may laugh and still resent you. Aim upward (institutions, systems, yourself) or sideways (shared inconveniences). The goal is solidarity, not superiority.

Keep It Clean

Avoid crude language, innuendo, and bathroom humor. It narrows your audience and shifts attention from your idea to your risk-taking. Clean humor travels: it works in boardrooms, classrooms, and contests without "translation."

Avoid High-Voltage Topics

Politics, religion, race, gender, body image, and tragedy are off-limits for off-the-cuff laughs. You don't know everyone's story in the room. Even a clever line can reopen wounds. When in doubt, respect the boundary.

Self-Deprecation—with Limits

A light poke at your quirks is endearing: it signals confidence and humility. But don't undermine your competence. "I'm forgetful" can be charming; "I'm hopeless" erodes credibility. Laugh at a moment, not your value.

Read the Room—and Your Role

Context governs consent. A playful remark may fit a club meeting but not a crisis briefing; fine for a keynote, wrong for a memorial. Your role matters too: the more authority you hold, the more careful your humor must be. Power amplifies both the laugh and the harm.

Timing and Tone

Humor belongs before or after gravity, not on top of it. If the room is grieving or tense with bad news, lead with empathy, not levity. Place lightness as a release valve *after* you've acknowledged the weight.

Consent, Callbacks, and Names

Never single out a person for a laugh without clear permission. If you callback something earlier, ensure it was universally received and kind. Use titles and names respectfully—clever is not a license to be casual.

Cross-Cultural Sensitivity

What's funny at home can be puzzling—or offensive—elsewhere. Avoid idioms, sarcasm, and local references that require insider knowledge. Prefer visual, situational, or universally human humor; it crosses borders cleanly.

Safety Checklist & Fail-Safe Exits

Ask: *Is it kind? Is it clear? Is it necessary now? Would I say it if a camera were rolling?* If any answer is "no," pivot. If a line misses, smile and move: "That one was just for me," or, "All right—back to the point." Graceful exits protect momentum and trust.

Used within these boundaries, humor unites, uplifts, and strengthens your message.

◇ ◆ ◇ ◆ ◇— ✦ — ✦ —◇ ◆ ◇ ◆ ◇— ✦ — ✦ —◇ ◆ ◇ ◆ ◇

"All the great speakers were bad speakers at first."

— Ralph Waldo Emerson

♥ Techniques for Instant Wit

Wit is not memorized comedy—it is quick perception shaped into playful response. The good news is that wit can be cultivated. With the right techniques, you can train your mind to notice openings and deliver humor that feels effortless, even under pressure.

Observation First

Quick wit begins with sharp observation. Pay attention to details others ignore: the squeak of a chair, a flickering light, a phone buzzing at the wrong time. Commenting lightly— "Even the lights are nervous about this question"—turns distraction into connection.

Exaggeration and Hyperbole

Stretch the truth just far enough to be funny without becoming absurd. "My first Impromptu answer was so short, I think it set a record for fastest failure." Exaggeration works because the audience recognizes the seed of truth inside the stretch.

Wordplay

Language itself provides humor. A pun or a flipped cliché can refresh a tired idea. "They told me to think outside the box, but I couldn't even find the box." The key is restraint: a quick twist delights; overuse drains.

Linking and Reframing

Take the question and link it to an unexpected image. Asked about persistence, you might say, "Persistence is like Wi-Fi—you keep reconnecting until it finally sticks." Linking familiar frustrations to new contexts surprises the audience and sparks laughter.

Reversal of Expectation

Flip the obvious. If asked, "Are you nervous?" reply, "Of course—I'd be

---

"Flexibility is the universal key that unlocks many seemingly impenetrable opportunities."

— Doctor Perspective™

worried if I wasn't." The humor comes from delivering the opposite of what listeners expect.

Borrowing from Life

Everyday conversations are training grounds for wit. Playful responses to friends, cashiers, or coworkers sharpen your reflexes. The more you practice light banter, the more easily wit will surface when the spotlight is on you.

Warmth over Sting

Above all, wit must be light, not sharp. Sarcasm often wounds; observation, exaggeration, and wordplay uplift. Think of wit as seasoning—enough to make the meal enjoyable, never so much that it overpowers the dish.

With practice, instant wit becomes instinct. Instead of freezing when something unexpected happens, you'll welcome it, knowing that the right remark can turn a moment of tension into a moment of shared laughter.

♥ Stories That Trigger Laughter

If wit is the sparkle of a single remark, stories are the floodlight. A humorous story has room to build tension, deliver surprise, and leave an audience laughing while still taking away a point. In Impromptu speaking, stories are especially powerful because they are elastic—you can stretch them for time or trim them to a few sentences without losing their punch.

Everyday Mishaps

The richest humor often hides in life's small accidents. Missing the bus, spilling coffee, locking yourself out—these are universal experiences. When told with self-awareness, they become instant comedy. *"I once rehearsed my Table Topic so thoroughly that I forgot every word when I stood up. That's when I realized preparation is useful, but recovery is essential."* Listeners laugh not because the mishap is unusual, but because it is familiar.

Embarrassing but Relatable Moments

Audiences love vulnerability—up to a point. A story about confusing names, wearing mismatched shoes, or answering the wrong question works because everyone has been there. These laughs are safe, warm, and humanizing. The speaker who can laugh at themselves teaches the audience it's okay to laugh at their own stumbles too.

Exaggerated Recollections

Take a small inconvenience and magnify it playfully. *"My first Impromptu answer was so bad I considered entering the Witness Protection Program."* Hyperbole works when the exaggeration is obvious and the audience recognizes the truth beneath the stretch.

Character Contrast

Humor thrives in conflict between opposites. The stern teacher and cheeky student, the no-nonsense boss and the nervous new hire, even your "past self" colliding with your "present self." Contrasts animate a story and make the laughter sharper because tension seeks release.

Physical Humor in Storytelling

You don't need slapstick, but a raised eyebrow, a mimicked stumble, or the shrug of your "younger self" deepens the humor. People laugh when they can see the scene, not just hear it. Impromptu speaking rewards small gestures that reinforce the story.

The Rule of Three for Comic Payoff

Many humorous stories follow a simple rhythm: build-up, twist, payoff. Three beats are enough: setup, complication, and resolution with a surprise. In Impromptu speaking, brevity is king, and this structure keeps humor lean while still delivering impact.

When you learn to tell short stories with humor, you move beyond one-liners. You weave laughter into narrative. That skill not only entertains but

◊ ♦ ◊ ♦ ◊— ♣ — ♣ —◊ ♦ ◊ ♦ ◊— ♣ — ♣ —◊ ♦ ◊ ♦ ◊

"A mediocre speech supported by all the power of delivery is more impressive than the most excellent speech without it."

— Quintilian

also cements your point in memory, leaving your audience amused, impressed, and connected to you long after you sit down.

♥ Humor Recovery When Jokes Fail

Every speaker who dares to use humor eventually faces silence instead of laughter. In Impromptu speaking, that silence feels louder because you have no script to fall back on. But failure in humor is not fatal. In fact, how you recover can leave an even stronger impression than if the joke had landed. Audiences admire resilience, and humor recovery demonstrates it.

Stay Calm, Stay Smiling

Your first defense is composure. If you look embarrassed, the audience feels secondhand discomfort. If you smile naturally, they feel reassured. A calm face signals, *"This is still going according to plan."* Even silence becomes less awkward when you own it.

Acknowledge Lightly

Naming the failure can flip the moment. Lines like, *"Well, that joke sounded better in my head,"* or *"That one was for me, not for you,"* often get the laugh the original line missed. The audience sees honesty, and honesty is always likable.

Keep the Flow Moving

The greatest danger is freezing. Acknowledge, then pivot quickly to your point. Lingering on the flop magnifies it. Moving forward shrinks it to a momentary blip. The faster you return to substance, the faster the audience follows.

Prepare Rescue Lines

Having a few generic rescue phrases ready can save you:

"I'll check back later to see if that one worked."

"Note to self: never take that one on tour."

"Don't worry, the serious part is better."

Even if used rarely, rescue lines provide psychological safety.

Shift into Seriousness

Another recovery option is to pivot into gravity. *"All jokes aside, the real issue here is..."* The sudden turn creates contrast, which grabs attention and often restores authority. Humor can fail, but sincerity almost never does.

Remember Audience Grace

Audiences usually want you to succeed. When a joke fails, most feel sympathy, not hostility. They root for your comeback. If you recover with poise, they may respect you more than if everything had gone smoothly.

In short, a failed joke is not a disaster—it is an opportunity. Recovery shows authenticity, adaptability, and strength under pressure. In Impromptu speaking, those traits matter as much as laughter itself.

JOURNAL
Write it Down Before It Escapes!

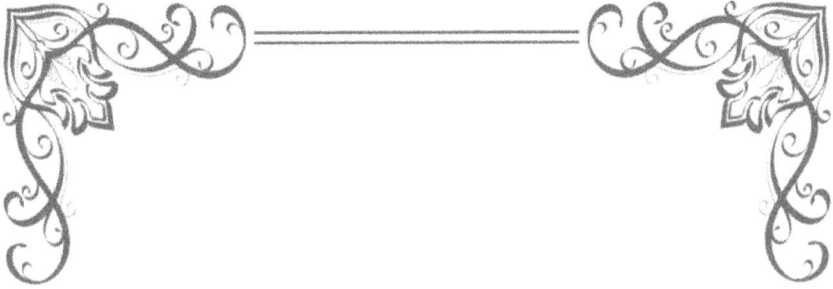

Chapter 8

Mastering Transitions: Turning the Unexpected into Flow

Look out for...

47) *Master Transitions: Turning the Unexpected into Flow*

48) *Good transitions signal direction. They tell the audience where you're going and why it matters*

49) *For the speaker, transitions provide breathing room.*

50) *Turn distractions into examples. If a door slams, you might say, "That's the sound of a closed opportunity—but here's the lesson: windows open."*

51) *Pick any topic—coffee, traffic, teamwork. Force yourself to speak for sixty seconds using a different transition each time*

♥ The Role of Transitions in Impromptu Speaking

If ideas are bricks, transitions are the mortar that holds them together. Without them, even strong content feels disjointed. In Impromptu speaking, where thoughts are generated on the spot, transitions become even more vital. They are the glue that prevents your audience from feeling as though they are listening to fragments instead of a message.

Why Transitions Matter More in Impromptu

Prepared speeches allow for rehearsed flow. Impromptu answers do not. When you are thinking aloud, the risk of jumping from one thought to another without connection is high. Transitions keep the audience with you by bridging the gap between those thoughts. A single phrase— *"Another way to see this..."*—can make the difference between sounding scattered and sounding polished.

Transitions as Signposts

Good transitions signal direction. They tell the audience where you have been, where you are, and where you are going. Think of a GPS: *"We've just passed Main Street, now we're heading to Oak Avenue."* In speaking: *"That's the challenge—but here's the opportunity."* Clear transitions guide listeners through your journey.

Transitions as Pauses for the Mind

For the speaker, transitions provide breathing room. They let your brain catch up. Saying, *"On the other hand..."* buys a second of time to shape the next sentence. Rather than panicking in silence, you appear deliberate. For the audience, the pause signals that a new point is about to unfold.

Emotional Transitions

Transitions are not only logical; they are emotional. You can move from seriousness to hope, from humor to reflection, from problem to solution. These emotional pivots keep your delivery dynamic.

"Delivery, delivery, delivery."

— Demosthenes (reported by Quintilian)

Imagine answering a tough question with a moment of levity, then transitioning smoothly: *"All jokes aside, the heart of the matter is this..."* The humor relaxes, the transition resets, and the gravity lands.

Everyday Examples

Politicians use transitions constantly: *"Yes, that's a challenge—but it's also an opportunity."* Teachers rely on them: *"Now that we've looked at history, let's connect it to today."* In each case, the transition prevents whiplash and creates flow.

Transitions are not decoration. They are navigation.

In a corporate pitch meeting, one manager stumbled through scattered points, leaving executives confused. Another, with fewer ideas, used simple transitions: *"Here's the problem... here's our plan... here's the benefit."* The second speaker won funding, not because of more content, but because transitions made the argument sound coherent.

Think of rivers: without tributaries joining smoothly, water floods chaotically. With channels and bends, it flows powerfully to its destination. Transitions are the bends and channels in your speech, directing energy instead of letting it scatter.

In Impromptu speaking, transitions make the difference between a talk that feels jagged and one that feels like a journey with an identifiable destination.

♥ Types of Transitions

Transitions come in many forms, and mastering them gives you flexibility. Each type serves a different purpose—some clarify logic, others shift emotion, and others simply buy you a moment of breath. Knowing the categories equips you to choose the right one on the spot.

Additive Transitions

These build momentum by stacking ideas. Words like *"also," "in addition,"* or *"another angle"* tell the audience you are adding, not replacing. Example: *"Courage builds leaders. In addition, compassion sustains them."* Additive transitions expand scope without losing focus.

Contrastive Transitions

These highlight differences. Phrases like *"however,"* *"on the other hand,"* or *"yet"* alert listeners to tension or balance. Example: *"Technology connects us instantly. Yet it can also isolate us if misused."* Contrast keeps your delivery balanced and thoughtful.

Teachers often rely on contrastive transitions to help students see nuance: *"Some historians say the empire collapsed from invasion; others argue it was internal decay. The truth lies in both."* Without that transitional framing, lessons feel like isolated facts instead of a connected narrative.

Causal Transitions

When you want to show cause and effect, use phrases like *"because of this,"* *"therefore,"* or *"as a result."* Example: *"The team lost trust, and as a result, productivity dropped."* These transitions make reasoning clear and strengthen persuasion.

Sequential Transitions

These mark order: *"first,"* *"next,"* *"finally."* Simple but powerful, they provide structure in contests or interviews where time is short. Example: *"First, preparation. Second, practice. Third, perseverance."* Sequential markers create rhythm and clarity.

Roman orators mastered sequential transitions. Cicero often organized arguments with *primo, secundo, tertio,* signaling listeners exactly where they were. Two thousand years later, the same devices remain effective.

Illustrative Transitions

Sometimes you need to move into a story. Use phrases like *"for example,"* *"imagine this,"* or *"picture a moment."* Example: *"We all know failure. Imagine standing onstage and forgetting every word."* This shifts abstract into concrete.

❋❋❋❋❋❋❋❋❋❋— ❦ — ❦ —❋❋❋❋❋❋❋❋❋❋

"Impromptu stories must be trimmed because the 'devil' is in the detail. Blame brevity on the lack of time."

— Doctor Perspective™

Emotional Transitions

These shift tone. Phrases like *"all jokes aside," "on a serious note,"* or *"beneath the laughter lies a truth"* pivot energy smoothly. They are invaluable when moving from humor to gravity or from tension to hope.

Conversational Transitions

In casual settings, softer phrases like *"by the way," "speaking of which,"* or *"that reminds me"* feel authentic. They keep you approachable without sounding scripted.

By mastering these types, you stock your mental toolbox with bridges for any terrain. Instead of abrupt jumps, you guide your listeners step by step, thought by thought, emotion by emotion.

♥ Transition Devices and Phrases

Knowing the *types* of transitions is the theory. Having a ready bank of actual phrases is the practice. In Impromptu speaking, you rarely have the luxury of inventing elegant wording under pressure. Stocking a set of versatile devices gives you something to reach for instantly—short, simple bridges that work in almost any situation.

Logical Connectors

These signal reasoning clearly. Examples:

"Because of this..."

"Therefore..."

"This leads us to..."

They make your progression sound deliberate, even when you're thinking on your feet.

Additive Phrases

Use these when layering multiple points.

"Not only that..."

"Along with this..."

"Equally important..."

They tell the audience you are building, not rambling.

Contrast Markers

Perfect for showing balance or acknowledging another side.

"On the other hand..."

"Still, we must consider..."

"Yet the opposite is also true..."

They prevent your answer from sounding one-dimensional.

Time Sequencers

These create order and rhythm.

"First... Second... Third..."

"A moment ago... Now... Next..."

"Before I close..."

They work especially well in interviews or contests where clarity is scored.

Illustrative Shifts

Move from abstract to concrete with:

"For example..."

"Imagine this..."

"Let me paint a picture..."

These turn concepts into experiences.

Emotional Pivots

When changing tone:

"All jokes aside..."

"On a serious note..."

"Behind the laughter lies a truth..."

These allow you to move smoothly between humor, gravity, and inspiration.

Conversational Fillers (Safe Ones)

Instead of "uh" or "um," try:

"You know..." Tone of voice here is critical. It must not sound lke a filler.

"Here's the thing..."

"That reminds me..."
They buy time without signaling panic.

Advanced Linking Devices

In a Table Topics contest, one competitor froze midway. She smiled, said, *"If we step back for a moment, what this really shows us is resilience,"* and flowed forward. That one transitional phrase salvaged the speech and earned her second place. The power wasn't in content—it was in a device used confidently.

When you want to sound especially polished:

"What this really shows us is..."

"If we step back for a moment..."

"The larger lesson here is..."
These elevate casual answers into mini-speeches.

Transitions are like neural synapses. Thoughts, like electrical impulses, must leap gaps. Without neurotransmitters—our verbal "because," "for example," "next"—the signal dies. With them, ideas fire smoothly, and understanding continues.

Memorize a handful in each category and rotate them in practice. Over time, they become instinctive, like reflexes. Instead of freezing between ideas, you'll glide from one to the next, keeping your audience engaged and convinced that you always know where you're going.

♥ Relay Questions: Passing the Baton Smoothly

Some Impromptu challenges don't end with you. In a relay-style setting—where one person answers, then hands off to another—the transition is not just helpful, it's mandatory. A clumsy handoff can break flow and leave the next speaker scrambling. A graceful transition, however, makes you look collaborative and confident.

~~~~~~~~~~~~~ •••••••• ~~~~~~~~~~~~~

"It is not enough to know what we ought to say; we must also say it as we ought."

— Aristotle

Case Example (Club): One participant was asked about teamwork. She ended her response with, *"But that's just my view—let's hear how Daniel has handled teamwork in his workplace."* The baton passed seamlessly, and Daniel didn't have to invent an entry point.

Case Example (Workplace): In meetings, managers often "tag" a colleague mid-discussion. The ones who prepare their transition— *"From the technical side, Maria can speak to the details"*—signal respect and aware-ness, while clumsy pass-offs create awkwardness.

The principle is simple: whether in a contest, a classroom, or a confer-ence call, your answer doesn't have to be the final word. Sometimes the most skillful move is to set up the next voice.

♥ Handling Interruptions and Curveballs

Even the best transitions face stress-tests: interruptions, unexpected questions, or sudden shifts in audience mood. In Impromptu speaking, these moments can rattle confidence if you are unprepared. But with the right strat-egies, you can not only survive interruptions—you can use them to strengthen your presence.

Pause Before You Pivot

When interrupted—by laughter, applause, or even a phone ringing—the instinct is to rush. Instead, pause. Smile. Let the moment breathe. Then bridge back: *"As I was saying..."* or *"That interruption actually proves my point..."* A calm pause shows mastery.

Acknowledge the Curveball

Pretending the interruption didn't happen makes you look detached. A brief nod to reality humanizes you: *"Looks like even the microphone has an opinion."* Recognition earns goodwill. Once acknowledged, redirect smoothly to your message.

Use Transition Stock Phrases

Curveballs demand quick pivots. Phrases like:

"That's a fair point—yet consider this..."

"Yes, and here's another perspective..."

"Interesting—let's connect that back to..."

These allow you to absorb the blow and redirect momentum without losing composure.

Reframe the Interruption as Content

During a press briefing on a natural disaster, a reporter's microphone failed with loud static. Instead of flinching, the spokesperson smiled: *"That noise is how it feels in our control room right now."* The crowd laughed, tension broke, and the official regained control. A disruptive curveball became an amplifier of credibility.

Turn distractions into examples. If a door slams, you might say, *"Life's interruptions are just like that—loud, sudden, and survivable."* Audiences admire speakers who improvise with what reality hands them.

Stay Flexible in Frameworks

Frameworks help under pressure, but interruptions may force you to compress. If a three-point PREP won't fit after a disruption, pivot to a single illustration and close decisively. The audience remembers flow, not format.

Guard Emotional Tone

A seasoned tennis player doesn't win every rally, but they reset quickly after each miss. Likewise, the Impromptu speaker doesn't need perfection— they need recovery. Transitions after interruptions are the mental footwork that keep you in the match.

The real danger of curveballs is not the distraction but your reaction. Irritation, sarcasm, or visible frustration erodes trust. Warmth, patience, and humor preserve authority. People forgive interruptions; they rarely forgive arrogance.

~~~~~~~~~~~~~~ ●●●●●●● ~~~~~~~~~~~~~

"If it is possible to cut a word out, always cut it out."

— **George Orwell**

Practice with Manufactured Distractions

Train by creating chaos: answer questions while music plays, while someone interjects, or while a timer buzzes. The more you rehearse under stress, the less rattled you'll be in real life.

Interruptions are inevitable; panic is optional. With composure, acknowledgment, and quick pivots, you can transform curveballs into opportunities—moments that prove not just your fluency, but your unshakable control.

♥ Practicing Fluidity Under Pressure

Fluid transitions in Impromptu speaking don't happen by accident. They are the product of deliberate training that conditions your brain to glide from thought to thought under stress. Just as athletes drill footwork until it becomes reflex, speakers must rehearse transitions until they become instinct.

Structured Drills

Pick any topic—coffee, traffic, teamwork. Force yourself to speak for one minute, but with a rule: every 10–15 seconds, insert a transition. Use a variety: additive (*"and another factor is..."*), contrastive (*"on the other hand..."*), illustrative (*"for example..."*). This exercise trains flexibility and prevents you from leaning on one device too often.

Countdown Practice

At a Toastmasters club in Toronto, members run a drill called "Ping-Pong Transitions." One speaker starts with a topic, and every 20 seconds, another member shouts "switch." The speaker must use a transition phrase to pivot instantly. Over weeks, participants report greater ease with both fluidity and audience trust.

Set a timer for decreasing intervals: 60 seconds, then 45, then 30. Each time, give an Impromptu response with clear transitions. The shrinking window forces you to connect ideas quickly without rambling.

Over time, you'll learn that even in 15 seconds, a clean transition makes your answer sound complete.

Partner Toss

Work with a friend or coach. Let them interrupt you mid-sentence with random words or questions. Your job: acknowledge, pivot, and resume smoothly. This strengthens your ability to recover from curveballs without losing composure.

Video Self-Review

Record yourself answering three Impromptu questions. Watch with the sound off first—did your facial expressions and pauses suggest control or panic during transitions? Then rewatch with sound—did your words flow or did they stall? Honest review accelerates growth.

Borrowing from Other Arts

Think of jazz musicians. They improvise freely, yet transitions between instruments feel seamless because each player listens for cues. In nature, migrating birds change direction mid-flight without chaos because transitions—tiny shifts in wingbeats—signal the flock. In both music and flight, fluidity under pressure comes from practiced responsiveness.

Actors practice improvisation games to sharpen spontaneity. Musicians drill scales so transitions between notes are seamless. Borrow their methods: join an improv class, rehearse vocal drills, or read aloud while inserting deliberate transitions. Each cross-discipline practice sharpens fluidity under pressure.

Building Mental Playlists

Create a list of your favorite transitional phrases and practice weaving them into answers. Over time, they become automatic—your brain pulls them out like a playlist on shuffle.

Fluidity is not about sounding rehearsed. It's about sounding effortless. With disciplined practice, your transitions will disappear into the flow of your message, leaving the audience with the impression that you were born speaking smoothly, even though every bridge was built through repetition.

◇♦◇♦◇— ♣— ♣—◇♦◇♦◇— ♣— ♣—◇♦◇♦◇

"Make practice a habit, not an event."

— **Doctor Perspective™**

JOURNAL
Write it Down Before It Escapes!

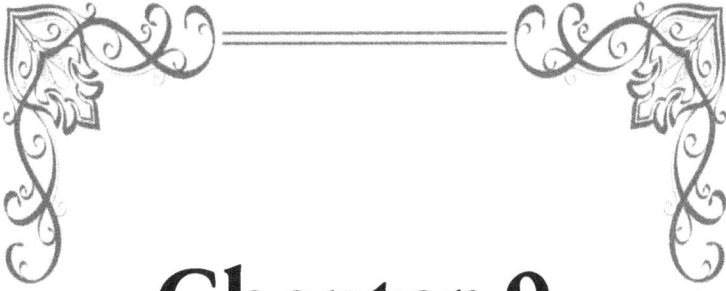

Chapter 9

Voice, Tone, and the Music of Spontaneity

Look out for...

52) *The human voice is the most flexible instrument.*

53) *In Impromptu speaking, vocal variety is not decoration—it is persuasion.*

54) *A personal story told with lowered tone and softened pace creates intimacy.*

55) *The silence itself becomes a vocal tool.*

56) *Audiences respond instinctively to shifts in volume, pace, and pitch.*

57) *Flat delivery, by contrast, dulls neural response.*

58) *Students lean forward, drawn into a story rather than a lecture.*

59) *The difference was not data but delivery.*

60) *Teachers who use vocal shifts hold attention longer.*

Vocal Variety as a Persuasive Tool

The human voice is the most flexible instrument on earth. It can whisper like a breeze, thunder like a storm, or carry warmth like a fire on a cold night. In Impromptu speaking, vocal variety is not decoration—it is persuasion. Words alone rarely persuade; it is how those words are delivered that determines whether they are believed, felt, and remembered. A flat voice turns diamonds into gravel, while a dynamic voice turns even simple stones into jewels.

Why Variety Matters

Audiences respond instinctively to shifts in volume, pace, and pitch. Neuroscientists note that monotony reduces attention within seconds, while variation reawakens the brain. A strong point delivered with rising pitch, slower pace, and deliberate pauses seizes attention. A personal story told with lowered tone and softened pace creates intimacy. The voice is the bridge between intellect and emotion; without variety, your content may be correct, but it will not connect.

The Science of Vocal Impact

This principle is not only intuitive—it is measurable. Neuroscientists confirm what great speakers already practice: vocal variety activates both hemispheres of the brain. Rising pitch and faster tempo stir energy and urgency; slower pace and softened tone create empathy and intimacy. When your voice modulates, the audience's brain quite literally lights up in different regions. Flat delivery, by contrast, dulls neural response. In the courtroom, classroom, or conference hall, a well-timed pause or tonal shift does not just color the words—it amplifies persuasion itself.

✳✳✳✳✳✳✳✳✳✳— ♣ — ♣ —✳✳✳✳✳✳✳✳✳✳

"What is written without effort is generally read without pleasure."
— **Samuel Johnson**

Practical Application

Pitch Ladder Exercise: Read a neutral line (e.g., "Today is Tuesday") three times—once in a low, serious tone, once in a mid-level conversational tone, and once at a higher pitch with enthusiasm. Notice how meaning shifts without changing the words.

Pace Control Drill: Record yourself answering a short Impromptu question. Play it back and mark where you rushed or dragged. Rehearse again, deliberately inserting one slow phrase and one fast burst for emphasis.

Pause Practice: Deliver a one-minute answer and force yourself to pause twice—once for impact, once for thought. The silence itself becomes a vocal tool.

Mirror Feedback: Practice in front of a mirror. Match your facial expression with vocal shifts so your tone and body language reinforce each other.

Case Study: The Boardroom Pitch

In a New York tech firm, two managers were asked to present competing proposals in the same meeting. One spoke in an even, unbroken monotone. His slides were sound, but his delivery felt lifeless, and executives tuned out. The second speaker, with fewer visuals, used contrast: speeding up with excitement when describing opportunity, slowing down and lowering pitch when describing risks, and emphasizing keywords by elongating syllables. The board approved her project unanimously. The difference was not data but delivery.

Classroom Illustration

Teachers who use vocal shifts hold attention longer. A history teacher explaining the fall of Rome might raise pitch to dramatize invading armies, then drop into a near-whisper to describe the crumbling senate. Students lean

※※※※※※※※※※— ♣ — ♣ —※※※※※※※※※※

"Gestures are not accessories. They are essential tools in your toolkit"

forward, drawn into a story rather than a lecture. The same principle applies in a 15-second Table Topic—if your voice rises, falls, speeds, and slows, your listeners will track you as though on a journey.

Cross-Domain Parallel: Nature and Music

Think of waves against the shore. They crash, recede, swell, and fall. That variation keeps us captivated. In music, monotony is noise; rhythm, rests, and crescendos are what make melodies memorable. The voice works the same way. Audiences crave patterns broken by surprise. Variety is the rhythm of persuasion.

Contest Example

In a Toastmasters Table Topics contest, one finalist froze momentarily. Instead of rushing, she used a long pause, lowered her voice, and said slowly, *"That silence... is the sound of fear."* The crowd erupted in applause. She transformed what could have been weakness into power through vocal variety.

Practical Application for Impromptu

When caught off guard, think: **pace, pitch, pause.** Speed up to energize, slow down to emphasize, rise to inspire, lower to reassure. Even in 15 seconds, these shifts create drama and persuasion.

The voice is not merely a carrier of words—it is the persuader itself. Master vocal variety, and even in an unprepared moment, you will sound intentional, convincing, and unforgettable.

♥ The Role of Tone in Shaping Meaning

If vocal variety is the music of delivery, *tone* is the emotional color of the message. The same sentence— *"I'm glad you're here"*—can sound sincere, sarcastic, affectionate, or dismissive depending on tone. In Impromptu speaking, where every second counts, tone often carries more meaning than the words themselves. An audience may forget what you said, but they will not forget how you made them feel.

Why Tone Outweighs Content

Psychologists studying communication patterns consistently find that a large portion of perceived meaning comes from tone rather than word choice. A firm, steady tone builds trust; a playful, rising tone sparks energy; a weary, flat tone drains the room. When words and tone clash—saying *"I'm confident"* with a shaky, apologetic tone—the audience believes the tone, not the text. This means that in Impromptu moments, shaping tone is not optional; it is the difference between credibility and collapse.

Case Study: A Courtroom Contrast

During closing arguments in a trial, one attorney recited strong facts but with a rushed, almost desperate tone. The jury sensed anxiety and discounted his logic. The opposing attorney, with less evidence, spoke slowly and with calm conviction. His tone projected confidence, and the jury awarded his side the verdict. The outcome was not decided by evidence alone, but by the emotional impression created through tone.

Classroom Example

A teacher answering a student's tough, skeptical question can either respond with irritation or with curiosity. Tone makes the difference. Irritation shuts students down; curiosity invites them in. In one university seminar, a professor who consistently responded with a warm, encouraging tone was rated far higher in "intellectual rigor" than another who used the same words but carried a condescending tone. Students equated warmth with wisdom.

Nature and Science Parallel

Tone is like the weather. The same landscape looks inviting under sunlight, ominous under storm clouds. Words are the terrain; tone is the sky above it. Similarly, brain-imaging studies show that tone activates emotional centers more quickly than content does, explaining why audiences "feel" tone before they parse meaning.

~~~~~~~~~~~~~~ •••••••• ~~~~~~~~~~~~~

"Proper words, in proper places, make the true definition of a style."

— **Jonathan Swift**

Contest Example

In a Table Topics contest, one speaker began with the words, *"This is a difficult question."* But instead of a defeated tone, she said it with a playful lilt, smiling as though in on a joke. The audience laughed, and she owned the moment. Her words admitted difficulty, but her tone framed it as opportunity.

Practical Application for Impromptu

Before you speak, ask yourself: *What emotional climate do I want to create?* Hope? Urgency? Calm? Then let tone lead the words. Use warmth for connection, gravity for authority, lightness for charm. A 15-second Impromptu answer can succeed or fail on tone alone.

Tone is the subtle but decisive tool of meaning. Words provide structure, but tone paints the picture, fills the space, and determines whether your audience walks away persuaded, comforted, or unmoved.

♥ Rhythm, Pauses, and Silence

If tone is the emotional color of speech, rhythm is its heartbeat. Every Impromptu response has a natural cadence, and mastering rhythm means guiding your audience's attention as deliberately as a conductor leading an orchestra. Pauses and silences are not gaps to be feared; they are instruments of persuasion. A well-placed pause can emphasize a point more powerfully than another sentence ever could.

Why Rhythm Matters

Listeners unconsciously sync with the rhythm of a speaker. Monotony lulls them into disengagement, while varied rhythm keeps them attentive. A quickened pace communicates excitement, urgency, or energy. A slowed, deliberate rhythm signals gravity and importance. Pauses punctuate like commas and periods in writing—they give structure and clarity. Without rhythm, even sharp content feels scattered.

※※※※※※※※※※— ♣ — ♣ —※※※※※※※※※※

"What is written without effort is generally read without pleasure."

— Samuel Johnson

Case Study: A Political Speech

During a campaign rally, one candidate delivered a string of policy promises with no rhythm—each sentence ran into the next. The words blurred. Another candidate, though less detailed, inserted pauses and varied her tempo. She allowed applause lines to breathe, punctuated critical promises with silence, and accelerated during calls to action. Analysts agreed that her rhythm, not her policies, made her speech memorable.

Classroom Example

In a literature lecture, a professor read Shakespeare with flat delivery. Students fidgeted and checked their phones. Another professor read the same passage but paused at dramatic turns and stressed key phrases with longer silence. The class leaned in, hanging on each word.

Rhythm made centuries-old text feel alive.

Nature and Science Parallel

Nature itself teaches rhythm. Waves crash and retreat; heartbeats thump and rest; birds call in patterns of sound and quiet. Neuroscientists confirm that human brains find patterned variation comforting and memorable. Silence allows neurons to encode the message more deeply. That is why speeches with pauses feel more profound—they literally give the brain time to absorb.

Contest Example

At a world championship of public speaking, a finalist began with a 10-second silence, simply looking at the audience. The pause, uncomfortable at first, drew every eye. When she finally spoke, the words carried weight far beyond their content. The pause had prepared the room to listen.

♥ Practical Application for Impromptu

When answering on the spot, embrace rhythm intentionally. Speed up to show enthusiasm; slow down to show reflection. Use pauses after key lines:

◇ ♦ ◇ ♦ ◇— ♣ — ♣ —◇ ♦ ◇ ♦ ◇— ♣ — ♣ —◇ ♦ ◇ ♦ ◇

"The safest humor is self-directed, not self-deprecating. When you deprecate yourself, your audience might just believe you."

— **Doctor Perspective™**

"The truth is... [pause] ...we are capable of more than we imagine." Silence is not failure—it is punctuation, drama, and power.

Mastery of rhythm, pauses, and silence transforms Impromptu speaking. It turns hurried thoughts into music, and fleeting moments into unforgettable impressions.

Exercises for Vocal Mastery

Vocal mastery is not reserved for actors or singers. Any Impromptu speaker can train their voice to become more dynamic, flexible, and persuasive. Just as athletes condition their bodies for peak performance, speakers can condition their vocal instruments. These exercises build strength, range, and control so that when the moment of pressure arrives, your voice performs reliably, not randomly.

Breathing as the Foundation

The voice begins with breath. Without control of airflow, volume and tone wobble. Practice diaphragmatic breathing: inhale deeply so your stomach expands rather than your chest, then release slowly on a steady exhale. Try reading a paragraph in one breath to strengthen endurance. In moments of stage fright, deep breathing also calms nerves, giving you both composure and power.

Warm-Up Routines

Professional speakers and singers rarely step on stage without warming up. Simple hums, tongue twisters, and lip trills loosen vocal cords. Even a two-minute routine—humming a scale, stretching the jaw, rolling the shoulders—sharpens resonance and clarity. In Impromptu contests, a brief warm-up before your name is called primes your instrument for precision.

♥ Case Study: The Courtroom Advantage

A trial lawyer in Chicago noticed that jurors leaned back when he raised his voice suddenly, mistaking passion for anger. Through daily breathing and modulation exercises, he learned to project intensity without harshness.

Within six months, colleagues noted that his closing arguments carried more conviction and less strain. The jury's response confirmed that vocal mastery changed outcomes.

Classroom Illustration

Elementary teachers often lose voices from constant speaking. Those who adopt posture and breath exercises sustain their vocal health and keep energy consistent all day. One teacher reported that varying pitch intentionally during story time not only preserved her voice but kept restless students captivated.

Nature and Science Parallel

Think of birdsong. Birds rarely deliver notes at one pitch; they modulate naturally, signaling attraction, alarm, or territory. Similarly, human voices evolved as signals of intention.

Training your voice to vary in pitch and pace taps into this primal communication, making you instinctively persuasive.

Contest Example

In a Toastmasters contest, one finalist used vocal drills to prepare for the unknown question. She practiced scaling from whispers to crescendos while articulating tongue twisters. On stage, when asked about resilience, she delivered her PREP with crisp enunciation and bold shifts in volume. Judges later remarked that her voice "commanded the room."

Practical Exercises

Pitch Ladder: Say the same phrase at five different pitches, from low to high.

Volume Contrast: Alternate between whispering and projecting the same sentence.

Pace Variation: Read a paragraph slowly, then again quickly, then mix both.

Mirror Drill: Record and play back your practice, noting how shifts affect impact.

Consistency is built in rehearsal, not performance. With regular exercises, your voice becomes reliable under pressure, capable of persuading, inspiring, or comforting on demand.

♥ Voice and Tone in Cross-Cultural Contexts

In a global world, Impromptu speaking often crosses cultural boundaries. A voice or tone that persuades in one setting can confuse—or even offend—in another. Mastery of cross-cultural vocal communication is therefore essential. It is not enough to control pitch, pace, and tone; you must also understand how those elements are *interpreted* by different audiences.

Why Cross-Cultural Awareness Matters

Tone carries assumptions. In some cultures, direct projection signals confidence; in others, it may be perceived as aggression. Silence may be respected as wisdom in East Asian contexts but misunderstood as uncertainty in parts of the West. A speaker who uses humor with a teasing tone in the United States may earn laughter, while the same tone in Germany may be judged as flippant. Understanding these nuances separates a merely competent Impromptu speaker from a truly global communicator.

Case Study: The Business Negotiation

In a multinational deal between an American firm and a Japanese company, the American executive relied on a fast pace and emphatic tone to project enthusiasm. His counterpart interpreted the delivery as pushy and insincere. A cultural consultant coached him to slow his rhythm, lower his pitch, and introduce longer pauses. The negotiation atmosphere shifted; respect grew, and the deal was signed. The change wasn't in content but in cross-cultural vocal adjustment.

Classroom Example

International classrooms illustrate these contrasts daily. A teacher from Latin America, accustomed to expressive vocal energy, may overwhelm Scandinavian students used to calmer delivery. Conversely, a soft-spoken Finnish

◊ ♦ ◊ ♦ ◊— ♣— ♣—◊ ♦ ◊ ♦ ◊— ♣— ♣—◊ ♦ ◊ ♦ ◊

"Not every question is neutral. Many are loaded double-barrel guns"

— **Doctor Perspective™**

lecturer may lose American students accustomed to higher energy. Both can adapt by moderating tone to suit the cultural listening environment without losing authenticity.

Nature and Science Parallel

Consider how animals adapt their calls in different environments. Birds in dense forests use slower, lower-pitched songs that carry through trees. Birds in open fields use faster, higher notes to travel across distance. Similarly, human voices adapt across "cultural environments." What carries weight in one cultural forest may vanish in another's open plain.

Contest Example

At a Toastmasters International contest, one speaker from India delivered with high speed and intensity. Some judges found it passionate; others found it overwhelming.

Another contestant, aware of the diverse audience, intentionally varied tone—mixing energized sections with quieter, reflective moments. Her adaptability won her the trophy, not because she was the most eloquent, but because she was the most universally accessible.

Practical Application for Impromptu

Research cultural norms if you know your audience.

Default to clarity: moderate pace, clear articulation, respectful tone.

Watch body language cues—leaning back, frowns, or laughter at odd moments signal misalignment.

Be willing to adjust in real time: slow down, soften tone, or add warmth as needed.

Cross-cultural vocal awareness is not about losing authenticity; it is about broadening range. The best Impromptu speakers sound at home in any room, whether that room is in Boston, Beijing, or Berlin.

JOURNAL

Write it Down Before It Escapes!

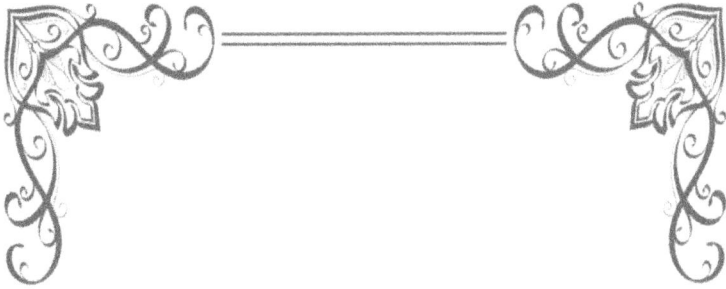

Chapter 10

Body Language That Speaks Before Words Do

Look out for...

61) *An upright, balanced stance communicates readiness, steadiness, and self-respect.*

62) *Students instinctively read posture.*

63) *Animals use posture to communicate long before vocal signals*

64) *Audiences sense authority in expanded posture and vulnerability in collapsed posture.*

65) *Gestures are not accessories. They are extensions of thought.*

♥ Posture as Presence

Long before you speak a word, your body has already delivered a message. Audiences make split-second judgments based on how you stand, sit, or enter the space. In Impromptu speaking, where you may not have the luxury of preparation or a polished script, posture becomes the first—and sometimes strongest—signal of credibility. The old saying *"actions speak louder than words"* is nowhere more visible than in posture.

Why Posture Matters

Psychologists studying nonverbal communication have found that posture accounts for a large percentage of how we interpret confidence and authority. An upright, balanced stance communicates readiness, steadiness, and self-respect. A slouched or collapsed posture signals fatigue, nervousness, or disinterest—even if your words are strong. In Impromptu moments, the audience may forget your points but they will not forget how you carried yourself.

Case Study: The Boardroom Interview

In a Fortune 500 company interview panel, two candidates faced rapid-fire questions. One hunched forward, clutching his notes. His answers were technically correct, but executives described him afterward as "hesitant." The second candidate sat tall, shoulders back, and leaned forward slightly when listening. Even when she paused to think, her posture conveyed composure. She won the position. Her edge wasn't vocabulary—it was presence.

Classroom Illustration

Students instinctively read posture. In one university debate, a participant delivered brilliant analysis but folded her arms tightly, sending signals of defensiveness. Her opponent, less articulate but standing open with arms relaxed at his side, received higher audience ratings. The lesson was clear: posture amplifies or undermines your message.

"A toolbox is never finished. As you grow, so do your tools."
— **Doctor Perspective™**

♥ Cross-Domain Parallel: Nature and Evolution

Animals use posture to communicate long before vocal signals. A lion standing tall with mane bristled intimidates rivals; a bird puffing its chest attracts mates. Humans share the same instincts. Audiences sense authority in expanded posture and vulnerability in collapsed posture. It is not cultural—it is biological.

Contest Example

At a Table Topics contest, one finalist froze when called. Instead of speaking immediately, she planted her feet firmly, stood tall, and breathed. The silence lasted three seconds, but the posture radiated authority. When she began, the audience was already with her. She did not earn applause for words alone—her posture set the stage.

Practical Application for Impromptu

Plant feet shoulder-width apart to signal stability.

Keep shoulders back but relaxed to signal calm authority.

Lean slightly forward when listening to show engagement.

Avoid fidgeting, slouching, or crossing arms unless intentional.

Posture is not cosmetic. It is presence embodied. In Impromptu speaking, where every second counts, your posture tells the audience: *"I belong here. You can trust me."*

♥ Your First Message Is Silent

Long before you speak, your body has already declared something. In an Impromptu setting, posture and presence form the unspoken first impression. Shoulders slouched, eyes down, or hesitant movements communicate uncertainty before a single word escapes your mouth. Conversely, upright posture, steady eye contact, and purposeful movement create an aura of credibility that primes the audience to listen.

Psychologists call this *thin slicing*—the human tendency to form judgments in the first few seconds. Audiences rarely wait for content to decide whether to trust you; they decide instinctively from what they see. Your body is your first speech.

Practical Drill

Posture Reset: Before speaking, plant both feet firmly, roll your shoulders back, and align your spine. Hold for three breaths. This becomes your baseline of confidence.

Eye Contact Triangle: When answering, look briefly left, right, and center, so no one feels excluded.

Controlled Movement: Step forward only when making a strong point; pause when delivering a conclusion. Movement then feels purposeful, not nervous.

♥ Gestures That Reinforce Points

Gestures are the body's exclamation marks, commas, and underlines. They add emphasis, illustrate meaning, and make ideas visible. In Impromptu speaking, gestures become critical because they clarify thought while projecting confidence. Without them, your words float unanchored; with them, your ideas are embodied. The audience not only hears you—they *see* you.

Why Gestures Matter

Communication researchers estimate that a majority of perceived meaning comes from nonverbal cues. Gestures occupy a central role in this. A well-timed hand movement can highlight a keyword, show contrast, or paint a mental picture. They also help the speaker. Physical movement organizes thinking, reduces anxiety, and anchors memory. A clenched fist signals conviction; open palms suggest honesty; a sweeping motion conveys scale.

Case Study: The Boardroom Presentation

During a corporate pitch, one executive clasped his hands tightly on the podium. His words were sound, but his rigidity conveyed fear. His competitor gestured naturally—palms open when inviting agreement, slicing motions when describing problems, circular movements when explaining processes.

"Good transitions signal direction. They are essential to effective mis-direction in humorous speech."

— Doctor Perspective™

Though his proposal was weaker on paper, his gestural fluency projected clarity and confidence. The board awarded him the contract.

Classroom Illustration

A high school teacher once explained democracy without gestures. Students described it as "dry." Later, she repeated the lesson, this time using her hands to mimic balance scales, a gavel, and open doors. Students recalled far more detail. The gestures imprinted ideas visually, turning abstraction into memory.

♥ Cross-Domain Parallel: History and Science

The great Roman orator Cicero trained not only in rhetoric but in controlled gestures. He believed a lifted hand, properly timed, could sway an audience as much as logic. Modern neuroscience supports him: hand movements activate visual processing areas in the brain, making information "stickier." Audiences literally remember more when they see gestures paired with words.

Contest Example

In a Table Topics contest, one speaker froze his arms at his side, fearing distraction. Judges marked him down for stiffness. Another speaker, nervous but animated, gestured to draw a circle in the air when describing "life's cycles." The audience nodded visibly. The point landed not because of the phrase but because the gesture illustrated it.

Practical Application for Impromptu

Use gestures that *match content*: upward for hope, downward for gravity, outward for inclusion.

Keep movements within the "gesture box"—shoulders to waist—so they feel controlled, not wild.

Avoid repetitive fidgeting (e.g., constant pointing or fiddling) that distracts more than it supports.

Rehearse by delivering responses in front of a mirror, checking if gestures look intentional and natural.

Gestures are not accessories. They are extensions of thought. When synchronized with words, they transform ideas from abstract to embodied. In Impromptu speaking, that embodiment persuades before logic has time to catch up.

♥ Eye Contact and Connection

The eyes are often called the "windows of the soul," and in Impromptu speaking, they are also the windows of credibility. Words may be polished, gestures may be smooth, but without genuine eye contact, audiences remain unconvinced. Eye contact bridges the unseen gap between speaker and listener, transforming a one-way speech into a dialogue—even when no words are exchanged.

Why Eye Contact Matters

Human beings are hardwired to interpret gaze. Neuroscientists have shown that direct eye contact activates areas of the brain linked to trust and empathy. Looking away too often signals nervousness, evasiveness, or insecurity. Sustained, balanced eye contact communicates confidence, honesty, and connection. In Impromptu speaking, where you cannot lean on notes or slides, the eyes must do double duty: keeping you anchored and keeping the audience engaged.

Case Study: The Job Interview

A young graduate faced an intimidating panel interview. His answers were correct, but he looked constantly at the table. Panelists later reported that they "didn't feel connected." Another candidate, with less polished answers, distributed steady eye contact across the panel, holding each person's gaze for a few seconds. Interviewers described him as "confident and trustworthy." He won the position. The deciding factor wasn't knowledge—it was connection through eyes.

Classroom Illustration

In a university setting, a lecturer noticed students drifting off during Impromptu discussions. She began intentionally scanning the room, meeting eyes with individuals while making key points. Students later reported feeling "included" and "seen." Attendance improved. The lesson was clear: eye contact is not only a delivery tool, but also a teaching strategy.

♥ Cross-Domain Parallel: Nature and Evolution

Animals use gaze to signal dominance, threat, or bonding. Wolves maintain eye contact to assert pack hierarchy. Infants bond with caregivers through prolonged gaze, building attachment. Humans inherit this instinct: when a speaker holds the audience's eyes, they command attention and foster trust.

Contest Example

At a Toastmasters contest, one finalist avoided eye contact out of fear, staring above the audience's heads. Judges marked him down for "disconnect." Another finalist, equally nervous, chose to hold brief but steady eye contact with individuals, moving naturally across the room. The audience leaned in as though spoken to personally. The second contestant advanced—not because of superior logic, but because his eyes communicated sincerity.

Practical Application for Impromptu

Sweep the room with **balanced gaze**: left, center, right, front, and back.

Hold contact with individuals for 3–5 seconds before moving on.

Use eye contact to emphasize points: lock eyes briefly during critical statements.

Avoid darting eyes, which suggest insecurity, or staring, which creates discomfort.

Eye contact is not just seeing—it is being seen. In Impromptu speaking, genuine eye connection transforms fleeting words into lasting impressions,

"Delivery has an extraordinarily powerful effect in oratory."

— Quintilian

building trust before logic has even begun its work.

♥ Facial Expressions as Amplifiers of Emotion

The human face is a canvas of emotion, capable of signaling joy, doubt, fear, excitement, and empathy in milliseconds. In Impromptu speaking, facial expressions often carry more weight than carefully chosen words. A single raised eyebrow can suggest skepticism, a gentle smile can disarm tension, and a furrowed brow can underscore seriousness. Where words may stumble under pressure, expressions fill the gaps, painting the message vividly for the audience.

Why Facial Expressions Matter

Research in psychology demonstrates that people are significantly more likely to believe a message when facial expressions align with the spoken words. If someone says "I'm thrilled to be here" with a blank face, the audience senses dishonesty. Conversely, a slight smile paired with sincerity creates warmth and trust. Expressions serve as instant feedback to the audience, confirming not only what you say but how you feel about it.

Case Study: The Business Pitch

During an investor pitch, one entrepreneur maintained a neutral, almost expressionless face while describing a groundbreaking idea. Investors interpreted his delivery as disinterest. Another entrepreneur, presenting a less innovative concept, smiled genuinely when describing potential impact and showed authentic concern when acknowledging risks. Her expressions reinforced her words, leading investors to fund her project. The lesson was clear: expression turned an ordinary pitch into a persuasive moment.

Classroom Illustration

A middle-school teacher explaining fractions with a flat face lost her students within minutes. When she tried again with wide eyes, animated smiles, and mock grimaces for mistakes, students leaned forward, laughed, and retained more information. Her content hadn't changed—her face had.

♥ Cross-Domain Parallel: Theater and History

Actors rely on facial expression to embody characters long before dialogue is delivered. Silent film legends like Charlie Chaplin captivated global audiences without sound, proving the universality of expression. Similarly, political leaders throughout history have shaped moments not just through words, but through visible emotion—Lincoln's grave solemnity at Gettysburg or Churchill's steely resolve during wartime broadcasts.

Contest Example

In a Table Topics contest, one speaker answered nervously with minimal expression, leaving judges uncertain of his conviction. Another finalist used her eyes, mouth, and brow dynamically—smiling warmly at the opening, tightening features in a moment of conflict, and relaxing with relief in conclusion. The second contestant won, proving that expressions can be decisive when content is equal.

Practical Application for Impromptu

Smile when appropriate; warmth builds rapport instantly.

Let eyes widen slightly to signal enthusiasm or wonder.

Use raised eyebrows to underscore curiosity or surprise.

Relax your face during reflective pauses to avoid appearing tense.

Avoid over-exaggeration, which can look theatrical rather than authentic.

Facial expressions are emotional punctuation marks. They clarify tone, amplify sincerity, and invite audiences to feel alongside you. In Impromptu speaking, where moments are short and stakes are high, your face often persuades before your words have the chance.

※※※※※※※※※※— ♣ — ♣ —※※※※※※※※※※

Whatever is true, whatever is noble, whatever is right, whatever is pure, whatever is lovely, whatever is admirable—if anything is excellent or praiseworthy—think about such things.

Philippians 4:8

♥ Synchronizing Voice and Body for Maximum Impact

The most powerful Impromptu speakers are not remembered for isolated strengths in voice or body, but for how the two flow together seamlessly. When voice and body reinforce one another, the message becomes unforgettable. When they clash—passionate words paired with lifeless posture, or bold gestures paired with timid tone—the message collapses. Synchrony is the hallmark of mastery.

Why Synchronization Matters

Audiences subconsciously check for alignment. When the body affirms what the voice says, credibility skyrockets. If a speaker says *"I am confident"* while standing tall, speaking steadily, and looking directly at listeners, belief follows. If the same words are mumbled with slumped shoulders and wandering eyes, belief evaporates. Consistency between channels—verbal and nonverbal—creates integrity in perception.

Case Study: The Leadership Rally

At a company rally, one executive delivered an urgent call for innovation. His words were fiery, but his body was rigid, and his voice flat. Employees described him afterward as "uninspiring." Another executive, using fewer words, varied her pitch and pace while gesturing broadly and leaning into the crowd. The audience reported being "energized." The content was secondary—the synchronization of voice and body carried the day.

Classroom Illustration

A science teacher explaining photosynthesis read monotonously from notes while drawing stiff diagrams. Students were bored. The next day, she explained the same process while gesturing with her arms like rays of sunlight and shifting her voice from soft (light entering leaves) to strong (sugar creation). Students later recalled the lesson more vividly, crediting "the way she showed it" rather than the words alone.

♥ Cross-Domain Parallel: Music and Dance

Consider how a violinist and dancer perform together. If the music soars while the dance lags, the performance feels broken. But when each movement matches the rhythm and tone of the music, the audience is transported. Voice is the music; body is the dance. In great Impromptu speaking, they move as one performance.

Contest Example

At an international speech contest, one competitor emphasized hope with her words but crossed her arms tightly. Judges marked her down. Another finalist said, *"We rise together,"* as she raised her arms and lifted her voice simultaneously. The crowd responded with a standing ovation. Synchrony turned good content into a moment of collective experience.

Practical Application for Impromptu

Match volume with gesture size: bigger gestures deserve stronger projection.

Use pauses in speech to align with stillness in body; movement during silence distracts.

Mirror emotional tone physically: soft voice with open palms, powerful voice with strong stance.

Practice in a mirror or on video to check alignment. Ask: *Do my voice and body tell the same story?*

Synchronization is not performance trickery—it is authenticity embodied. The best Impromptu speakers sound the way they look and look the way they sound. That unity persuades, inspires, and endures.

~~~~~~~~~~~~~ ●●●●●●●● ~~~~~~~~~~~~~
"Speed without wisdom is reckless."
— **Doctor Perspective™**

JOURNAL

Write it Down Before It Escapes!

※※※※※※※※※※※—✤—✤—※※※※※※※※※※※

Death and life are in the power of the tongue, and those who love it will eat its fruits.

Proverbs 18:21

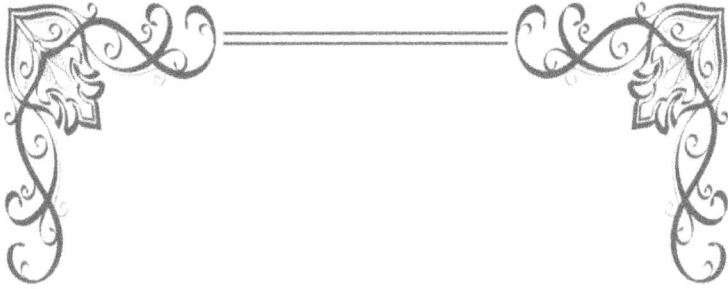

Chapter 11

Impromptu in Professional Life

Look out for...

66) *Wherever people think on their feet, they are engaging in Impromptu communication.*
67) *The ubiquity of Impromptu proves one truth: mastering it is not optional.*
68) *Teaching Impromptu is like conducting a live orchestra.*
69) *Courtroom advocacy is persuasion under pressure.*
70) *Leaders are constantly thrust into unscripted encounters.*
71) *Master the unscripted and you master the moment.*
72) *Every word counts, and every hesitation is magnified.*

♥ The Ubiquity of Impromptu in Professional Settings

Impromptu speaking is not confined to Impromptu Speech Club meetings, debate clubs, or speech contests. It appears in almost every professional arena, from classrooms and courtrooms to boardrooms and press briefings. Wherever people think on their feet, they are engaging in Impromptu communication. Understanding the universality of this skill reveals its value not just as a contest exercise, but as a professional survival tool.

The Professional Landscape

Teachers must field unexpected questions from students who may or may not be testing their knowledge. Lawyers must adjust instantly when judges interrupt their arguments with probing queries. Doctors must explain diagnoses and treatment options clearly when patients arrive with urgent, unfiltered concerns. Politicians must navigate reporters' rapid-fire questions in press conferences. Business leaders face Q&A sessions with investors or employees where every word is scrutinized. Each of these settings demands the ability to respond quickly, clearly, and persuasively without a prepared script.

Case Study: The Doctor's Diagnosis

A physician in a busy emergency room is asked by a patient's family member, "Is she going to be okay?" The question is urgent, emotional, and loaded. The doctor cannot read from a textbook. He must balance honesty with reassurance, technical accuracy with layman's clarity. This is Impromptu speaking at its highest stakes, where tone, body language, and word choice affect not only understanding but trust and emotional well-being.

Case Study: The Political Press Conference

When President John F. Kennedy held live press conferences, he rarely knew in advance what reporters would ask. His calm tone, quick humor, and ability to pivot from hostile questions to clear answers built his reputation as a confident leader. In today's world of instant media replay, the ability to respond Impromptu has become even more critical.

~~~~~~~~~~~~~~ •••••••• ~~~~~~~~~~~~~~

"Theory is only as powerful as practice."
— **Doctor Perspective™**

One misstep can dominate headlines for weeks; one sharp, credible answer can restore public trust.

♥ Nature and Science Parallel: Adaptability

In nature, survival often depends on adaptability. Consider the chameleon, able to shift its colors to fit the environment. Or consider how the human immune system rapidly produces antibodies to new viruses it has never "studied" before. Impromptu speaking is the professional equivalent: a skill of adaptive response in changing conditions. Just as adaptability ensures survival in nature, Impromptu speaking ensures survival in professional credibility.

Practical Application

Teachers: Rehearse explaining complex concepts in simple terms, as if a child had asked.

Lawyers: Practice summarizing a case in 30 seconds, ready for any judge's interruption.

Doctors: Develop analogies for medical terms so they are instantly available in patient conversations.

Executives: Rehearse clear, value-based answers to tough questions investors or employees might raise.

Impromptu speaking is the invisible thread binding professional life. Whether in the classroom, the courtroom, or the operating room, it is the ability to think, speak, and connect under pressure that defines credibility. The ubiquity of Impromptu proves one truth: mastering it is not optional. It is essential for every professional who leads, teaches, persuades, or reassures in real time.

♥ The Classroom: Impromptu as Teaching in Real Time

Nowhere is Impromptu speaking more visible than in the classroom. Teachers and professors live in a constant state of unprepared dialogue. They enter a lecture hall with a plan, but the plan must bend the moment a student raises a hand. A child might ask, "Why is the sky blue?" in the middle of a science lesson on gravity. A university student may challenge a historical interpretation with new evidence from an article they just read. The teacher cannot press pause, consult a book, and return later. They must answer in real time, balancing accuracy, engagement, and authority.

The Teacher's Tightrope

The classroom is an arena where the teacher's credibility is tested daily. A confident response to a curveball question strengthens authority, while hesitation or defensiveness weakens it. One high school teacher recalls a lesson on World War II when a student asked, "Could the war have been avoided if leaders had acted differently?" The teacher paused, acknowledged the depth of the question, and then gave a layered, thoughtful response. That moment became a turning point in how the class viewed her expertise. Her Impromptu skill reinforced her authority far more than her prepared lecture notes did.

Case Study: The College Seminar

In a political science seminar, a professor prepared to discuss constitutional law. A student raised a question about a breaking news event involving a Supreme Court decision. The professor had not planned for this, but he framed his answer by first clarifying the student's question, then connecting it to principles already covered in class. By bridging the unexpected with the planned, he not only answered the question but reinforced the course material. His Impromptu answer transformed distraction into teaching.

The Socratic Method: Structured Improvisation

The ancient Greek philosopher Socrates pioneered a style of teaching based almost entirely on Impromptu responses. Rather than delivering lectures, he asked probing questions and responded to answers with more questions. His method required the agility to guide conversation in real time, adapting to each student's response. This "structured improvisation" is still practiced in law schools today, where professors train future attorneys to

———+———+———✒✒✒✒✒———+———+———

"If I am to speak for ten minutes, I need a week for preparation; if an hour, I am ready now."

— Woodrow Wilson

think on their feet.

The Socratic method is proof that Impromptu speaking is not new—it is a timeless form of intellectual engagement.

♥ Cross-Domain Parallel: The Orchestra Conductor

Teaching Impromptu is like conducting a live orchestra. The conductor may have a score, but the performance is alive: a violin string breaks, a trumpet enters early, the acoustics shift with the crowd. The conductor cannot stop the performance. They adjust tempo, signal a section, or cover with a broader gesture. The show continues seamlessly. Likewise, teachers must adjust in real time, keeping the "music" of learning alive even when surprises occur.

Practical Application

Teachers: Anticipate potential student questions and practice short, clear explanations.

Professors: Link current events back to course themes, showing students that knowledge is living, not static.

Trainers: Use participant input as a springboard, rather than a distraction, to keep energy high.

Classrooms are not rehearsed speeches; they are living conversations. Teachers who master Impromptu speaking transform curiosity into learning, skepticism into dialogue, and interruptions into deeper engagement. The classroom is proof that Impromptu is not merely survival—it is the essence of true education.

♥ The Courtroom: Persuasion Under Fire

If the classroom is a testing ground for curiosity, the courtroom is a battlefield of persuasion. Every word counts, and every hesitation is magnified. Lawyers, judges, and witnesses are locked in a dynamic exchange where scripts dissolve quickly under the pressure of objections, interruptions, and unexpected testimony. Courtroom advocacy is one of the purest examples of Impromptu speaking under fire.

The Lawyer's Challenge

Attorneys may prepare opening statements and closing arguments for weeks, but cross-examination rarely follows a script. A hostile witness may provide a surprise answer; a judge may interrupt mid-sentence with a pointed question; opposing counsel may raise an objection that derails a carefully planned line of inquiry. In those moments, the lawyer's ability to pivot calmly and respond with precision determines whether the jury perceives confidence or collapse.

Case Study: Clarence Darrow

The legendary American lawyer Clarence Darrow was known not only for eloquence but for improvisation. In the famous Scopes "Monkey Trial" of 1925, Darrow faced a barrage of objections and hostile questioning. Rather than faltering, he reframed questions on the spot, turned pressure into persuasion, and used wit to expose weaknesses in the opposition. Historians note that his success lay not only in prepared arguments but in his ability to think aloud persuasively under relentless scrutiny.

Modern Example: The Courtroom Pivot

In a recent civil trial, an attorney questioning a witness was interrupted repeatedly by opposing objections. Instead of showing frustration, she smiled and reframed her question three different ways until it was allowed. The jury noticed her calm under pressure and rewarded her persistence with increased credibility. Her Impromptu adjustments mattered more than the specific question she asked.

♥ Cross-Domain Parallel: The Chess Master

Courtroom advocacy resembles a high-level chess match. A grandmaster may plan an opening, but each move by the opponent demands recalibration. No plan survives the game unchanged. Likewise, no attorney's script survives intact once the trial begins. The skill lies not in memorizing every move but in anticipating patterns and improvising with agility.

"Not every curveball deserves a full swing."

— **Doctor Perspective™**

Contest Illustration

Toastmasters Table Topics contests often simulate the courtroom dynamic: a speaker begins with one idea but must pivot rapidly when the question takes a turn. Just as a lawyer answers a judge while staying persuasive to the jury, a contestant answers the contest chair while connecting with the audience. Both require presence of mind and the ability to keep multiple audiences in focus at once.

Practical Application

Lawyers: Practice reframing questions three ways to anticipate objections.

Students of Law: Drill with unexpected hypotheticals to build reflexive clarity.

Speakers: Rehearse handling interruptions with grace rather than irritation.

The courtroom magnifies the stakes of Impromptu speaking. Words can determine freedom, guilt, or justice. Mastering Impromptu in this arena is not about cleverness alone—it is about steadiness, clarity, and the resilience to persuade under fire.

♥ The Boardroom and Beyond: Corporate Impromptu

If the courtroom is persuasion under pressure, the boardroom is persuasion under scrutiny. Corporate leaders, managers, and employees alike are constantly placed in situations where they must respond instantly—without the safety of slides, scripts, or lengthy preparation. Investor Q&A sessions, executive briefings, project updates, and job interviews all demand the ability to think aloud clearly while the stakes are high.

The Investor Pitch

Imagine a startup founder presenting to a panel of venture capitalists. The presentation ends, and one investor asks a blunt, unexpected question:

"Why should we believe you can execute this better than a competitor with more resources?" The founder's Impromptu answer will weigh more heavily than the rehearsed deck. A confident response—framed around unique strengths, team resilience, or early traction—can secure funding. A faltering or defensive reply can sink the deal.

Case Study: The Executive Briefing

In a Fortune 100 company, an executive was asked mid-presentation about a sudden downturn in quarterly profits. Instead of dodging, he paused, acknowledged the problem, and reframed it as an opportunity for innovation. His steady Impromptu framing reassured board members and employees alike. Analysts later noted that confidence in leadership rose, not because of the data itself, but because of the composure of the response.

Classroom Parallel

Corporate Impromptu moments often resemble the classroom dynamic. A teacher adjusting a lesson on the fly mirrors a manager adapting a presentation when an unexpected question arises. Both require agility, humility, and the ability to pivot without losing authority.

♥ Cross-Domain Parallel: Neuroscience of Decision-Making

Neuroscientists describe two systems of decision-making: System 1 (fast, instinctive, emotional) and System 2 (slow, deliberate, logical). In boardrooms, executives must bridge both systems—speaking quickly enough to show command, yet logically enough to satisfy scrutiny. Successful Impromptu speakers harness System 1 for speed while guiding their audience toward System 2 reasoning. This blend reassures listeners that quick answers are also thoughtful answers.

Contest Illustration

A Toastmasters Table Topics contest offers similar stakes in miniature. Contestants field an unexpected question in front of an audience, knowing judges score not just clarity but confidence. Corporate leaders experience the same scrutiny—except the "judges" are investors, employees, or media outlets whose decisions carry financial and reputational consequences.

Practical Application

Executives: Rehearse responses to hard questions about performance, vision, and competition.

Job Seekers: Practice clear, structured answers to "Tell me about yourself" or "Why should we hire you?"

Team Leaders: Use Impromptu drills in meetings, where each member answers a random question in 60 seconds.

The boardroom may lack the legal stakes of the courtroom, but the professional consequences can be just as high. Funding, careers, and reputations rise or fall on the ability to respond convincingly without warning. In business, as in law, Impromptu mastery is not a luxury—it is leadership in action.

Politics and Public Service: Speaking Without a Net

Few arenas demand more Impromptu skill than politics and public service. Leaders are constantly thrust into unscripted encounters—press conferences, town halls, interviews, legislative debates. Unlike the classroom or boardroom, where stakes are professional, here the stakes are often national or even global. Every spontaneous word is recorded, replayed, and judged by millions. In this realm, Impromptu speaking can secure trust or trigger crisis.

Press Conferences: The Ultimate Test

Press conferences strip leaders of control. Reporters ask unpredictable, often hostile questions. The speaker must answer in real time, balancing honesty with diplomacy. John F. Kennedy became a master of this art. His press conferences revealed quick wit and composure. When faced with aggressive questioning, he often diffused tension with humor before pivoting to substance. This Impromptu agility enhanced his reputation as a confident leader.

Case Study: The Mayor's Town Hall

At a city hall meeting, a mayor fielded angry questions about rising crime. One citizen shouted, "Why should we trust you—you've failed us be-

"Where observation is concerned, chance favours only the prepared mind."
— Louis Pasteur

fore!" The mayor paused, acknowledged the frustration, and reframed: "You are right to demand more. Here is what we are doing differently now." The Impromptu choice to validate emotion before presenting facts shifted the room from hostility to cautious hope. That moment was cited later as a turning point in his re-election campaign.

Legislative Debate: Thinking on the Floor

In legislative chambers, lawmakers often face surprise challenges from opponents. A senator may introduce an amendment on the spot. The ability to respond with a clear, persuasive argument in seconds is as critical as the content of the law itself. Those who falter appear uninformed; those who pivot with conviction win influence.

Cross-Domain Parallel: Tightrope Walking

Political Impromptu resembles walking a tightrope in public view. Each step must be steady, because one slip is magnified for all to see. Unlike private boardrooms, missteps here are instantly public and potentially career-ending. The skill is not just in balance but in the grace to recover if one foot slips.

Contest Illustration

Toastmasters contests, though far smaller in scale, mirror this environment. Contestants must deliver coherent, persuasive answers in front of judges and an audience. The audience may laugh, question, or even resist. The skill of connecting under scrutiny prepares leaders for the unforgiving spotlight of politics.

Practical Application

Public Officials: Anticipate hostile questions and rehearse empathetic yet firm responses.

Community Leaders: Validate emotions before presenting solutions.

Speakers: Train to deliver in high-pressure, on-camera settings where replay magnifies every slip.

Politics and public service amplify Impromptu speaking beyond professional settings. Words can shape public trust, sway policy, and alter history.

To speak without a net is to prove not only rhetorical skill but character under pressure.

Lessons Across Domains: Transferable Skills

The classroom, courtroom, boardroom, and political arena may seem like separate worlds, but they share a common thread: the demand for confident, persuasive Impromptu speaking. Whether a teacher explaining a sudden question, a lawyer handling an objection, a CEO addressing investors, or a politician answering a hostile reporter, the underlying skill is the same—thinking and speaking under pressure. The differences lie in context; the transferable skills lie in principle.

Common Threads

Across domains, we see recurring themes: the need to pause before responding, the ability to validate emotions, the discipline to pivot without panic, and the skill to project confidence even when caught off guard. A teacher who masters these habits in the classroom can carry them into corporate training. A lawyer who practices courtroom poise can excel in media interviews. The skill multiplies as it transfers.

Case Study: The Cross-Trained Professional

One executive began his career as a teacher, honing the ability to simplify complex ideas for restless students. Later, as a corporate leader, he used the same Impromptu clarity to field tough investor questions. He later entered public service, where his ability to validate emotion while delivering fact-based answers became his hallmark. His story demonstrates that Impromptu mastery in one setting prepares you for many others.

♥ Cross-Domain Parallel: Athletic Cross-Training

Athletes often improve by training outside their sport: basketball players run track to improve endurance, swimmers practice yoga for flexibility. The same principle applies to Impromptu speaking. A lawyer practicing in Toastmasters strengthens humor and presence; a teacher joining a debate club

✳✳✳✳✳✳✳✳✳✳— ♣ — ♣ —✳✳✳✳✳✳✳✳✳✳✳

"A well-timed pause is the secret sauce of humor."

sharpens argumentation. Skills gained in one arena create transferable strength across all others.

Contest Illustration

Toastmasters contests exemplify transferability. Members from diverse careers—engineers, educators, lawyers, entrepreneurs—step into the same spotlight. Each brings professional habits but gains new ones from the contest stage. When they return to their fields, they carry sharpened reflexes, broader perspective, and greater confidence.

Practical Application

Teachers: Join professional associations to practice Impromptu in unfamiliar contexts.

Lawyers: Attend community forums to translate legal jargon into accessible speech.

Executives: Teach or mentor to refine clarity and patience.

Politicians: Train in corporate or educational settings to strengthen empathy and structure.

Cross-Domain Reflection: The Value of Role Models

Across fields, one of the fastest ways to accelerate Impromptu growth is to observe experts outside your own profession. Teachers who study lawyers learn courtroom control. Politicians who watch stand-up comics learn timing and recovery. Executives who shadow teachers pick up clarity under constant questioning. The common thread is this: exposure multiplies skill. When you train your Impromptu instincts through varied role models, you gain versatility that no single field can teach.

~~~~~~~~~~~~~~ ●●●●●●●● ~~~~~~~~~~~~~~
"The pause is not hesitation; it is orchestration."
— Doctor Perspective™

Case Example:

A senior manager preparing for media interviews began attending an Impromptu Speech Club. By stepping into the shoes of educators and debaters, he learned to simplify complex information into clear, relatable points. Later, he testified before Congress, where his ability to pivot without notes earned bipartisan praise. His story illustrates how skills sharpened in one arena can transfer into even the highest-stakes environments.

The most valuable lesson is this: Impromptu speaking is not confined to one profession. It is a universal skill, transferable across domains. Those who practice it deliberately find themselves better prepared for life's unexpected questions, no matter the setting.

JOURNAL
Write it Down Before It Escapes!

✳✳✳✳✳✳✳✳✳✳— ♣ — ♣ —✳✳✳✳✳✳✳✳✳✳

"Plans are worthless, but planning is everything."

— **Dwight D. Eisenhower**

Chapter 12

Owning the Mic Without a Script: Media, Podcasts, etc.

Look out for...

73) *Every word counts, and every hesitation is magnified.*

74) *Cross-training builds resilience and agility*

75) *Virtual Impromptu is the new normal*

76) *Without Impromptu agility, a speaker can ramble, lose focus, or appear unprepared.*

77) *Unlike a lecture hall, podcast listeners can disengage instantly with a tap.*

78) *The ability to thrive in this landscape requires Impromptu mastery not only to answer but to engage.*

79) *A podcast host expects you to answer questions conversationally.*

The Rise of Unscripted Media

In the modern era, communication has shifted dramatically from polished, rehearsed speeches to spontaneous, unscripted interactions. Podcasts, live streams, radio interviews, and panel discussions have exploded as platforms where thought leaders, professionals, and ordinary individuals reach massive audiences. Unlike a keynote address where slides and notes guide delivery, unscripted media requires the speaker to perform Impromptu in real time. Every word, tone, and gesture is amplified by microphones, cameras, and the permanent record of digital playback.

♥ Why It Matters

Audiences today crave authenticity. They no longer want distant experts reading from scripts; they want human connection through dialogue. A podcast host expects you to answer questions conversationally. A panel moderator may throw an unexpected challenge your way. A live-stream audience may send comments in real time, shifting the direction of the conversation. The ability to thrive in this landscape requires Impromptu mastery not only to answer but to engage.

When speakers falter or rely too heavily on pre-rehearsed lines, listeners often sense the disconnect. Authentic presence cannot be manufactured—it emerges in the unscripted moments when a leader speaks candidly, responds with vulnerability, or adjusts their language to connect with the heartbeat of the audience. The rise of unscripted media has therefore redefined authority: it is no longer measured by polish alone, but by responsiveness under pressure.

Case Study: The Viral Podcast Moment

Consider the CEO who appeared on a widely followed podcast to discuss leadership. Midway through, the host asked, "What was your biggest failure, and how did you recover?" The CEO had not prepared for this vul-

◊ ♦ ◊ ♦ ◊—♣—♣—◊ ♦ ◊ ♦ ◊—♣—♣—◊ ♦ ◊ ♦ ◊

"Preparation, I have often said, is rightly two-thirds of any venture."

— Amelia Earhart

nerable question.

Instead of dodging, he shared a candid story about a failed product launch, adding humor and a lesson learned. The clip went viral, generating more positive press than his polished press releases ever had. That unscripted moment became the centerpiece of his brand.

Another striking case came from an Olympic athlete interviewed immediately after a disappointing performance. Instead of repeating bland talking points, she admitted her frustration, then pivoted to highlight lessons learned about resilience. Her tears, combined with her candid reflection, spread across social media and inspired millions. That raw moment built credibility in ways no scripted message could.

♥ Cross-Domain Parallels

Impromptu speaking in media is like jazz performance. Jazz musicians may begin with a theme, but the real magic happens when they riff, respond to other players, and adapt to the flow of the moment. In podcasts and panels, the same principle applies. Prepared talking points set the key, but the improvisation around those points creates the music that resonates.

We can also see parallels in the natural world: think of a flock of birds adjusting direction mid-flight, or a school of fish pivoting in unison when threatened. Their survival depends not on rigid pre-planning but on collective adaptability. In human communication, adaptability is equally critical—what matters is how fluidly the speaker adjusts to changes.

Practical Application

Executives: Anticipate tough or vulnerable questions in podcasts and prepare flexible frameworks, not memorized lines.

Panelists: Practice jumping into conversations midstream without derailing flow.

Podcasters/Hosts: Balance structure with improvisation, allowing genuine connection.

Leaders: Build resilience by practicing under simulated high-pressure Q&A scenarios.

♥ The Podcast Arena: Conversational Authority

Podcasts have become the dominant form of long-form unscripted media. Unlike television interviews that run for a few minutes, podcasts often last an hour or more, offering a platform for deeper conversations. This length creates opportunities—but also risks. Without Impromptu agility, a speaker can ramble, lose focus, or appear unprepared.

The Power of Conversational Tone

Podcast audiences expect intimacy. Listeners tune in during commutes, workouts, or quiet evenings, often through headphones. The guest's voice is literally in the listener's ear, creating a personal connection. An Impromptu misstep is not easily forgiven because the tone of authenticity is the contract between host and audience.

Tone also determines memorability. A monotone delivery, even with solid content, risks fading into background noise. By contrast, a warm, varied tone keeps listeners engaged for the duration. Unlike a lecture hall, podcast listeners can disengage instantly with a tap. The responsibility lies with the guest to sustain connection minute by minute.

Case Study: The Scientist Turned Communicator

A climate scientist once appeared on a popular podcast. Known for dense research papers, he was challenged by the host to explain his findings "as if to a 12-year-old." Instead of stumbling, he drew on metaphors: "Imagine the Earth wearing a thick blanket, and every year we add more layers so it can't cool down." That Impromptu analogy spread widely on social media and was later cited in congressional hearings. The scientist's credibility rose, not because of his research alone, but because of his spontaneous clarity.

Another memorable case came from a comedian-turned-activist guest. Asked about a complex policy issue, he paused and said, "It's like trying to fix a leaking roof during a storm—you've got to stay calm, patch what you can, and keep moving."

The metaphor was spontaneous, humorous, and relatable. That one line was quoted in newspapers and reposted across platforms, demonstrating how the podcast format rewards quick, creative phrasing.

Cross-Domain Parallels

Podcasting resembles a dinner table conversation among friends. It is informal, responsive, and adaptive. Just as one would shift tone when talking to a child versus an adult at dinner, podcast speakers must adjust based on the host's energy and the audience's needs.

It also mirrors therapy sessions: in counseling, a professional cannot script every response but must listen carefully, adapt language, and meet the client's needs in real time. Similarly, podcast guests must attend closely to the host's questions and emotional cues, responding with empathy as much as expertise.

In nature, bees provide a useful metaphor. As they communicate through a "waggle dance" to convey information about food sources, they adapt direction and intensity based on immediate need. So too must podcast speakers—adjusting emphasis and storytelling direction based on the flow of conversation.

Practical Application

Guests: Prepare stories and metaphors that simplify your expertise into everyday language.

Hosts: Ask open-ended questions that invite improvisation rather than rehearsed answers.

Speakers: Practice explaining your work without jargon, as if to a curious teenager.

———— ✦ ———— ✦ ————🐝🐝🐝🐝🐝———— ✦ ———— ✦ ————

"Fear thrives in the absence of structure."

— Doctor Perspective™

Professionals: Record mock podcast sessions to practice conversational agility under time constraints.

♥ Panels: Speaking in the Chorus

Panel discussions are increasingly popular in conferences, summits, and virtual events. They offer audiences the benefit of multiple perspectives at once. But for speakers, they pose unique Impromptu challenges: limited airtime, unpredictable dynamics, and the need to collaborate while standing out.

The Panelist's Dilemma

On panels, speakers cannot control the timing or flow. A moderator may skip you for a round, leaving you to jump in later. Another panelist may deliver your planned point before you speak. You must be able to reframe, pivot, and contribute fresh insights without repetition or defensiveness. Failing to do so risks fading into the background or sounding redundant.

Case Studies: Adaptability in Action

At a technology conference, a panelist prepared to discuss funding challenges for startups. Another panelist, speaking first, covered nearly all of his points. Instead of repeating, he said, "Building on that..." and shifted the conversation to the emotional toll on founders, using a personal story. His improvised pivot not only distinguished him but made the panel memorable.

Another example occurred at a health summit. A physician expected to discuss hospital infrastructure but was asked instead about personal resilience during the pandemic. She responded with an anecdote about her first exhausting months on the front lines, connecting it back to systemic weaknesses. Her honesty and flexibility drew the loudest applause.

♥ Cross-Domain Parallels

Panels resemble relay races: each speaker carries the baton briefly before passing it on. Dropping the baton—by going off-topic, hogging time, or repeating others—hurts the team. Strong panelists know when to run fast, when to slow down, and when to pass cleanly, keeping the race engaging.

They also parallel ecosystems in nature. Within a coral reef, each species has a niche role, and when one overpowers the rest, the ecosystem collapses. Likewise, panels thrive when each participant plays their part with balance.

In music, a panel discussion resembles a jazz ensemble. Each soloist contributes, but listening and responding to the others is just as vital as one's own performance. Harmony emerges only when individuals adapt to the group's rhythm.

Practical Application

Panelists: Listen actively and frame contributions as "building on" or "adding a new dimension."

Moderators: Direct questions strategically to balance airtime and avoid dominance by a single speaker.

Speakers: Practice concise, impactful answers that land in under two minutes.

Organizers: Encourage pre-panel collaboration so participants can anticipate overlaps and identify complementary angles.

Panel mastery means being agile, concise, and additive. The goal is not only to shine individually but also to elevate the conversation as a whole. When handled with skill, panels become more than a series of speeches—they become living dialogues that audiences remember.

♥ Sharpening Clarity Through Panels

In panel discussions, many speakers fall prey to what psychologists call the *spotlight effect*—the false belief that every tiny slip is magnified under audience scrutiny. In truth, most listeners are tracking the flow of ideas, not every stutter or filler word. Recognizing this truth frees you to focus on clarity rather than perfection.

※※※※※※※※※※— ♣ — ♣ —※※※※※※※※※※

"Practice is nine tenths."

— **Ralph Waldo Emerson**

Panels are unique because they demand brevity without sacrificing substance. Each answer competes with others, so the discipline of condensing your thought into 30–60 seconds trains you to strip away excess. The skill carries into boardrooms, classrooms, and even interviews: once you can deliver a crisp, memorable thought in a crowded conversation, solo speaking feels easier.

♥ Case Study: The Cross-Trained Communicator

One executive described how weekly podcast interviews sharpened her clarity for high-stakes board presentations. She called it "intellectual interval training." Podcasting taught her to hit strong points in 30-second bursts, while strategy sessions stretched her endurance. Each format built transferable muscle for the other. The result: she became both sharp under pressure and sustained under scrutiny.

Practical Application

Treat panels and podcasts as low-stakes laboratories for refining clarity.

Record one of your answers. Replay it and ask: *Could someone quote this back easily?* If not, refine.

Rotate practice between short-form (podcasts, panels) and long-form (speeches, briefings). Cross-training builds resilience and agility.

♥ Live Broadcasts and Breaking News: Thinking on Air

Live television and radio amplify the risks of Impromptu speaking. Unlike podcasts or panels, where editing is sometimes possible, live broadcasts offer no safety net. Every hesitation, stumble, or slip of the tongue is instantly transmitted to millions. Professionals who excel in these contexts combine preparation with the agility to respond in real time.

The On-Air Pressure

Broadcasters and guests must deliver concise, accurate, and engaging answers under strict time limits. Producers signal countdowns, anchors interject, and breaking news may shift the topic mid-sentence. A steady, confident response demonstrates authority, while visible panic erodes trust.

Case Studies: Composure Under Fire

During a natural disaster, a governor was interviewed live about relief efforts. Reporters asked about missing resources and political accountability. Instead of appearing defensive, he calmly acknowledged the challenge, gave specifics about next steps, and reassured citizens. His Impromptu composure under pressure boosted public confidence.

Another case occurred during a financial crisis when a central bank chair was asked live on-air about potential bank collapses. With markets watching, he avoided panic by calmly explaining protective mechanisms in place, using clear metaphors about "shock absorbers" and "safety nets." His unscripted steadiness prevented further market freefall.

Cross-Domain Parallels

Speaking on live media resembles walking a tightrope without a net. Every step must be deliberate, and recovery from missteps must be graceful. The ability to focus under scrutiny is the essence of balance, both literal and rhetorical.

A scientific parallel is the emergency room surgeon. Like live media spokespeople, surgeons cannot pause for lengthy deliberation; they must act swiftly and confidently with lives on the line, explaining their choices clearly to their team in real time.

In nature, the cheetah provides another parallel. Its survival depends on making split-second adjustments while hunting. A small miscalculation risks losing the prey. Likewise, in live broadcasts, quick yet controlled adjustments determine success.

Practical Application

Spokespeople: Rehearse sound bites that deliver clarity in under 30 seconds.

~~~~~~~~~~~~~ •••••••• ~~~~~~~~~~~~~

"Framework fluency is what makes you look not rehearsed, but responsive."

— Doctor Perspective™

Leaders: Practice pivoting from hostile questions to constructive answers.

Guests: Keep answers structured: acknowledge, inform, reassure.

Professionals: Simulate live interviews to build confidence under time pressure.

Mastery of live media lies not in avoiding risk but in embracing it—turning the pressure of the moment into an opportunity to project calm, clarity, and credibility.

♥ Virtual Media: Streaming, Webinars, and Interactive Q&A

Virtual platforms like Zoom, YouTube Live, and LinkedIn webinars have created new spaces for Impromptu speaking. Unlike traditional media, virtual spaces include interactive elements—chat boxes, live polls, and audience interruptions—that require multitasking in real time.

The Virtual Challenge

Speakers must split attention between the camera, the audience, and the constant flow of digital feedback. A poorly handled question or technical hiccup can derail authority. Strong Impromptu speakers prepare frameworks but stay agile enough to respond authentically in the moment.

The added complication is technology itself. Audio delays, camera freezes, and screen-sharing errors are almost inevitable. What distinguishes a confident professional is not the absence of glitches but the poise shown in handling them. A speaker who laughs off a frozen screen and pivots smoothly to voice-only mode often earns more goodwill than one who panics.

Case Studies: The Digital Crucible

A CEO hosted a global livestream for employees. In the chat, one worker anonymously asked, "Why should we trust leadership after last year's layoffs?" Instead of ignoring it, the CEO acknowledged the pain, outlined a vision for stability, and thanked employees for resilience. The candid, unscripted exchange became the defining moment of the town hall.

At a university webinar, a professor's slides failed to load. Instead of stalling, she drew a diagram on paper and held it to the camera while narrating. Students later reported that this improvised response made the lesson more memorable than the prepared slides would have.

♥ Cross-Domain Parallels

Managing live virtual Q&A resembles air traffic control—multiple signals coming at once, requiring prioritization and calm responses. Just as controllers ensure safety despite chaos, speakers must project order and focus amidst digital noise.

We might also compare virtual speaking to conducting an orchestra remotely. The conductor must keep tempo even as sound reaches musicians at slightly different times. In the same way, a webinar speaker must maintain rhythm despite lags and distractions.

Nature offers another parallel: the octopus, capable of moving its arms semi-independently while staying coordinated. Virtual presenters, too, must handle independent inputs—chat questions, visual slides, body language—while projecting unified coherence.

Practical Application

Hosts: Prepare a moderator to filter audience questions and manage chat flow.

Speakers: Keep a flexible outline while allowing interaction to guide depth.

Leaders: Treat tough digital questions as opportunities for transparency.

◇ ♦ ◇ ♦ ◇— ♣ — ♣ —◇ ♦ ◇ ♦ ◇— ♣ — ♣ —◇ ♦ ◇ ♦ ◇

"No plan survives first contact with the enemy."

— Helmuth von Moltke

Teams: Rehearse "failure drills" where technology intentionally breaks so everyone practices calm improvisation.

Virtual Impromptu is the new normal. Those who practice it not only survive technical chaos but thrive in it, proving their resilience and relatability to audiences worldwide.

♥ The Transferable Media Mindset

What unites podcasts, panels, broadcasts, and virtual platforms is the mindset required: openness, adaptability, and credibility under scrutiny. While formats differ, the principles of Impromptu speaking remain constant—listen actively, respond authentically, and guide conversations with composure.

Common Threads

Authenticity: Listeners forgive imperfection but not insincerity.

Clarity: Short, structured answers resonate in every format.

Connection: Eye contact with the camera, acknowledgment of audience energy, and tonal warmth build trust.

Authenticity comes not from flawless delivery but from honest presence. In an age of filters and polished corporate messaging, the unguarded moment often carries more persuasive weight than rehearsed brilliance. Clarity matters because attention spans are limited; the listener should be able to summarize your point in one sentence. Connection is forged when speakers acknowledge not only questions but the emotions behind them.

Case Studies: Transferability in Action

A leadership coach appeared on a podcast, then a panel, later a live CNN broadcast, and finally a LinkedIn webinar. Each required different adjustments, but the same core skill—Impromptu adaptability. Across all formats, her reputation grew as a trusted, authentic voice.

Another example: a young entrepreneur, inexperienced with media, faced a tough on-air critique of his business model. He responded with humility, admitting weaknesses but highlighting customer loyalty. Later, he was invited onto a podcast, where he deepened his story, then a virtual panel, where he refined his message. By the time he gave a keynote, he had built credibility through repeated Impromptu trials.

♥ Cross-Domain Parallels

Water adapts to any container yet remains fundamentally the same. Media Impromptu requires the same versatility—whether in a glass (podcast), a river (panel), or an ocean (broadcast). The shape changes, but the essence remains.

We might also think of seeds carried by the wind. They land in varied soil conditions—rocky, fertile, arid—but their internal blueprint allows them to grow wherever they settle. Similarly, transferable Impromptu skills root themselves in any medium and flourish according to the environment.

In sports, consider the all-around athlete. A decathlete competes in running, throwing, and jumping. The context changes, but core fitness and adaptability carry through. The Impromptu communicator is the decathlete of public speech, able to thrive across platforms.

Practical Application

Speakers: Train across multiple formats to expand agility.

Professionals: Review recordings of yourself to identify verbal tics or tone issues.

Leaders: Develop media presence as a transferable leadership asset.

Teams: Debrief after every media appearance to extract transferable lessons.

※※※※※※※※※※— ♣ — ♣ —※※※※※※※※※※

Death and life are in the power of the tongue, and those who love it will eat its fruits.

Proverbs 18:21

In every media format, Impromptu mastery is not accidental. It is the result of preparation, practice, and the ability to lean into unscripted moments with confidence. Those who own the mic without a script extend their influence across audiences and platforms alike.

JOURNAL
Write it Down Before It Escapes!

"Audiences perceive spontaneity as authenticity."
— **Doctor Perspective™**

Chapter 13

High-Stakes Leadership Moments: Impromptu for Influence

Look out for...

80) *In leadership, the moments that define reputations rarely arrive with a script.*

81) *High-stakes settings heighten the consequences of Impromptu communication.*

82) *A slip of the tongue can trigger market reactions, diplomatic tension, or organizational unrest*

83) *A thoughtful, composed response, even if imperfect, builds trust.*

84) *Curveball questions resemble surprise weather in sailing.*

85) *Audiences perceive spontaneity as authenticity.*

86) *A leader who pauses before speaking signals control.*

Leadership Under Pressure: Why Impromptu Matters Most

In leadership, the moments that define reputations rarely arrive with a script. They erupt in boardrooms when crises break, in press conferences when probing questions strike, or in town halls when frustrated employees demand answers. These are high-stakes leadership moments, where the ability to think and speak Impromptu determines whether trust is built or shattered. Leaders are not remembered for how they read prepared remarks but for how they respond under fire, when silence is not an option and every word carries weight.

♥ The Pressure of the Spotlight

High-stakes settings heighten the consequences of Impromptu communication. A slip of the tongue can trigger market reactions, diplomatic tension, or organizational unrest. Yet when leaders speak with clarity, empathy, and decisiveness in unscripted moments, they can calm fears and inspire confidence. The pressure itself becomes a crucible, revealing authenticity and resilience.

One reason Impromptu moments loom large is because they strip away polish. Audiences perceive spontaneity as authenticity. A carefully scripted answer may impress, but a thoughtful unscripted response convinces. Neuroscience research shows that authenticity activates trust regions in the brain—people instinctively sense when words are real. Thus, leadership Impromptu is not decoration but survival.

Case Studies: Defining Leadership by Words

The Corporate CEO in Crisis: After a product recall, a CEO addressed the media. Rather than hide behind technical jargon, she spoke plainly, accepted responsibility, and promised transparent updates. Her unscripted honesty salvaged customer trust.

※※※※※※※※※※— ♣ — ♣ —※※※※※※※※※※

"Master the unscripted and you master the moment."

— **Doctor Perspective™**

The Military Commander: When a mission failed, the commander had to brief grieving families. His improvised words acknowledged loss, honored sacrifice, and reaffirmed commitment. The speech, though unplanned, became a source of healing.

The Mayor in Disaster Response: Following a hurricane, a mayor fielded spontaneous questions on live television. By balancing empathy ("we hurt with you") with practical action steps, she projected competence and humanity.

The Tech Entrepreneur: In a live podcast, a founder was asked about layoffs. She admitted the difficulty but reframed it as an opportunity for innovation, offering concrete examples. Her candor turned critics into allies.

♥ Cross-Domain Parallels

Impromptu leadership under fire resembles a pilot handling turbulence mid-flight. Training provides the framework, but the actual response must be immediate, adaptive, and calm. In nature, lions demonstrate similar resilience when protecting their pride—instinctively decisive in the face of threats. Scientists describe such moments as "stress inoculation": organisms that survive shocks adapt and grow stronger. Similarly, leaders who face unscripted trials build resilience for future crises.

History provides parallels too. Abraham Lincoln's off-the-cuff remarks at Gettysburg initially seemed brief and improvised, yet became immortal. Winston Churchill's wartime speeches, often delivered with minimal notes, illustrate how spontaneous conviction can mobilize nations.

Practical Application

Leaders: Rehearse "crucible drills"—practice answering hostile or emotional questions without preparation.

Organizations: Develop culture where transparency is valued so leaders can speak candidly.

Teams: Support leaders by providing real-time data and emotional backup to reinforce improvised decisions.

Speakers-in-training: Review recordings of past Impromptu moments to analyze strengths and weaknesses.

♥ **The Power of the Pause in Leadership**

In high-stakes leadership moments—whether addressing a crisis, fielding a hostile question, or responding to sudden news—the most powerful word may be silence. A leader who pauses before speaking signals control. The pause creates space for thought, calms tension, and forces others to lean in. In contrast, leaders who rush to fill silence with filler or defensiveness often appear rattled.

Case Study: Boardroom Calm

During a volatile shareholder meeting, one CEO faced a barrage of accusations. Rather than fire back instantly, she paused, took a breath, and deliberately restated the central concern before answering. The room quieted. The pause reframed her as thoughtful rather than reactive, strengthening her credibility.

Practical Application

When confronted with a tough question, count "one, two" silently before speaking.

Restate the question in your own words. This buys time and ensures clarity.

Use a pause mid-answer to highlight your key point—leaders are remembered for what they emphasize.

Why This Matters

In leadership, Impromptu speaking is rarely about perfect phrasing. It is about presence under fire. Pausing converts chaos into composure, transforming a potential stumble into a defining moment of trust.Crisis Communication: Words That Steady the Storm

~~~~~~~~~~~~~ •••••••• ~~~~~~~~~~~~~
"Brevity is the soul of wit."
— William Shakespeare

Crisis strips leadership down to its essence. In those moments, employees, citizens, or stakeholders look to a leader's words for stability. Impromptu speaking in crisis is not about polished delivery but about conviction, honesty, and empathy. The wrong words can magnify fear; the right words, even if unpolished, can restore order.

♥ The Anatomy of Crisis Impromptu

Crisis responses must achieve three things quickly: acknowledge the reality, demonstrate empathy, and outline immediate action. A leader who denies, deflects, or delays loses credibility. By contrast, a leader who says, "Here's what we know, here's what we're doing, and here's how we care for you" builds trust, even if the situation remains fluid.

A critical factor is tone. Neuroscience shows that people under stress mirror the emotional cues of leaders. Calm words slow panic; frantic tone accelerates it. Effective crisis leaders consciously project steadiness even when internally uncertain.

Case Studies: Words in the Eye of the Storm

Corporate Scandal: A tech CEO confronted allegations of misconduct in a live Q&A. He began by acknowledging failures, then emphasized reforms. His unscripted sincerity lowered tensions and gave employees reason to stay.

Public Health Emergency: During a sudden outbreak, a minister faced the press. Without a script, she framed her remarks around shared humanity: "We are all vulnerable, but together we will protect the most at risk." Her calm tone steadied public morale.

Sports Example: A coach, after a devastating championship loss, spoke Impromptu to fans. Instead of excuses, he highlighted the team's resilience and future goals, transforming disappointment into loyalty.

Natural Disaster Response: A governor, facing flash floods, improvised updates on evacuation plans. By clearly repeating instructions and pairing them with compassion, she saved lives and reassured citizens.

Financial Crisis: A central banker, ambushed with questions about currency collapse, improvised metaphors to explain safeguards: "Think of our reserves as shock absorbers." His words prevented investor panic.

♥ Cross-Domain Parallels

Crisis Impromptu resembles a firefighter directing people out of a burning building: there's no time for lengthy explanation, only clarity and reassurance. In science, think of a doctor explaining emergency procedures mid-operation: concise, calm, and decisive. In nature, elephants in danger form a protective circle around their calves—an instinctive but clear signal of leadership and care.

History parallels abound. Franklin Roosevelt's unscripted fireside chats during the Depression exemplified calm in chaos. Jacinda Ardern's Impromptu remarks after tragedy in New Zealand demonstrated how empathy can stabilize a nation.

Practical Application

Leaders: In crisis, default to honesty over perfection. Practice drills where only 30 seconds are given to explain a complex situation.

Teams: Equip leaders with quick facts they can deploy in unscripted remarks. Train staff to provide "soundbite clarity" under pressure.

Organizations: Train spokespeople to acknowledge uncertainty without panic: "Here's what we know, here's what we're finding out." Encourage leaders to emphasize care as much as data.

Communicators: Develop analogies in advance so they are ready in emergencies.

♥ Negotiation and Diplomacy: Speaking Without a Net

Negotiation rooms and diplomatic summits are arenas where unscripted communication decides outcomes. While preparation sets the foundation, ac-

~~~~~~~~~~~~~~ ●●●●●●●● ~~~~~~~~~~~~~~

"Brevity signals clarity and respect."

— **Doctor Perspective™**

tual exchanges demand Impromptu agility. Every counterproposal, objection, or unexpected remark must be met with composure and strategy.

The Nature of Negotiation Impromptu

Negotiations test a leader's ability to balance firmness with flexibility. Too rigid, and opportunities are lost; too pliant, and credibility erodes. Impromptu speaking bridges this gap by allowing leaders to adjust tone, vocabulary, and strategy in the moment while holding to core objectives. Neuroscience research confirms that adaptive framing under stress activates problem-solving centers of the brain, enabling leaders to pivot creatively without losing authority.

Case Studies: Negotiation on the Edge

Diplomatic Summit: A foreign minister, caught off guard by a surprise proposal, reframed the discussion in real time to protect her nation's interests while avoiding escalation. She drew from shared values and avoided inflammatory language, earning respect.

Corporate Merger Talks: A CEO, confronted with an unexpected objection, improvised a new benefit structure that kept the deal alive. Instead of rejecting the objection, he validated it and reframed the terms.

Union Bargaining: A school superintendent, challenged publicly by union leaders, acknowledged valid concerns before pivoting to shared goals, defusing hostility.

Historical Example: At Camp David in 1978, Jimmy Carter improvised daily to bridge gaps between Menachem Begin and Anwar Sadat, reframing proposals in ways each side could accept. His Impromptu flexibility shaped a lasting peace accord.

Entrepreneurial Negotiation: A startup founder, unexpectedly challenged by investors, shifted metaphors mid-pitch: "We are not selling software, we are building a bridge to efficiency." That unplanned reframing unlocked funding.

♥ Cross-Domain Parallels

Negotiation Impromptu is like a chess match where not every move can be predicted. Players must adapt strategy on the fly. In the natural world, wolves negotiate territory: they signal strength but avoid wasteful fights, relying on adaptive cues. In science, think of molecules forming bonds: alignment shifts dynamically, but stable compounds emerge. In sports, consider basketball point guards improvising plays in real time—balancing vision and reaction.

Practical Application

Leaders: Practice "surprise drills" where unexpected counterpoints must be addressed live.

Teams: Prepare modular arguments leaders can draw from as needed. Create a library of persuasive metaphors.

Organizations: Train negotiators to reframe on the spot: "What I hear is X, but let's consider Y."

Professionals: Review famous negotiations and role-play with improvised objections.

♥ Inspirational Moments: Speaking to Hearts, Not Just Minds

Not all high-stakes leadership moments involve crisis or negotiation. Some are opportunities to inspire—funerals, celebrations, sudden calls to rally people. Here the Impromptu word becomes a torch, lighting paths forward.

The Anatomy of Inspirational Impromptu

These moments demand authenticity and emotional resonance more than eloquence. Listeners don't remember every phrase but how they felt. A spontaneous, heartfelt tribute often outweighs a carefully crafted script. Impromptu inspiration works because it bypasses analysis and connects directly to shared human experience.

Neuroscience shows that emotional resonance releases oxytocin, enhancing empathy and trust between speaker and audience.

Case Studies: Words That Inspired

National Mourning: A president, at a vigil, spoke off-script, quoting scripture and sharing personal grief. The brief, heartfelt words unified a grieving nation.

Graduation Speech: A school principal, with no notes, drew on personal anecdotes to encourage resilience in students. The authenticity moved families more than polished speeches.

Sports Locker Room: A captain, after an injury, rallied teammates with raw honesty: "This setback won't define us—we'll rise." The speech became legendary.

Civil Rights Leadership: Martin Luther King Jr.'s "I Have a Dream" speech contained improvised sections, including the famous refrain. Those unplanned words electrified the crowd and became history.

Faith Gathering: A pastor, speaking spontaneously after a community tragedy, set aside notes and prayed aloud. The vulnerable, unprepared words brought comfort far beyond the congregation.

♥ Cross-Domain Parallels

Inspirational Impromptu resembles a spark lighting dry tinder: small but transformative. In science, it is like a catalyst triggering a chain reaction, turning potential into energy. In nature, think of a dawn chorus of birds: unplanned, diverse, yet profoundly uplifting. In history, think of moments like Churchill's off-the-cuff encouragements during bombings, which galvanized resilience more than policy documents.

Practical Application

Leaders: Share personal stories, not clichés, in unscripted inspiration. Speak from lived experiences rather than prepared scripts.

Teams: Encourage moments where members speak authentically to each other, strengthening bonds beyond formal reports.

Organizations: Recognize that informal words often carry more cultural weight than formal policies. Build rhythms for spontaneous encouragement in meetings and gatherings.

Speakers-in-training: Practice telling a story unscripted, focusing on emotion rather than perfection.

♥ Ethical Leadership: Speaking When Silence Fails

Some of the most critical leadership moments occur when leaders must address ethical failures or injustices. Silence in such cases is complicity. Speaking Impromptu with integrity signals courage and sets moral direction.

The Weight of Ethical Impromptu

Addressing ethical lapses requires a balance of candor and vision. Leaders must acknowledge wrongs without equivocation while guiding toward restoration. These are not rehearsed moments—they demand moral clarity in real time. Ethical Impromptu is powerful because it shows that integrity is not a pre-written performance but a lived conviction.

Case Studies: Ethics on Display

Corporate Misconduct: A CFO, questioned about accounting irregularities, admitted mistakes and pledged reforms in an Impromptu board address. His honesty prevented shareholder revolt.

◊ ♦ ◊ ♦ ◊— ♣ — ♣ —◊ ♦ ◊ ♦ ◊— ♣ — ♣ —◊ ♦ ◊ ♦ ◊

"Speak clearly, if you speak at all; carve every word before you let it fall."

— Oliver Wendell Holmes Sr.

Social Injustice: A mayor, facing public protests, departed from prepared remarks to acknowledge systemic failures and commit to reforms. The shift from defensiveness to candor defused tensions.

Faith Leadership: A pastor, confronted mid-sermon with a congregant's question about hypocrisy, paused and answered candidly, sparking a church-wide renewal.

Historical Example: When Mahatma Gandhi was unexpectedly asked by journalists about colonial injustice, he spoke offhand: "My life is my message." That unscripted declaration became a timeless ethical compass.

Sports Administration: A league commissioner, asked spontaneously about discrimination in athletics, abandoned his notes and promised reforms on the spot. The Impromptu statement set a tone of accountability that formal policy later confirmed.

♥ Cross-Domain Parallels

Ethical Impromptu resembles a lighthouse in a storm: steady, visible, guiding others to safety. In law, it mirrors a judge giving off-the-cuff instructions that shape justice. In nature, it is the alpha elephant leading the herd through drought—not because of force, but trust. In science, it resembles the moment of chemical catalysis—one small spark shifts the entire reaction toward clarity and direction.

History also shows ethical Impromptu in action. Abraham Lincoln's spontaneous words in debates or Martin Luther King Jr.'s unprepared lines during marches shifted moral landscapes. Their credibility rested not on polish but conviction.

Practical Application

Leaders: Prepare not only facts but values to speak from in unscripted ethical dilemmas. Build a vocabulary of conviction that surfaces under pressure.

"Omit needless words."
— William Strunk Jr.

Teams: Support leaders with frameworks that emphasize transparency and fairness. Encourage immediate acknowledgment of wrongs instead of deferral.

Organizations: Celebrate Impromptu moral clarity as much as planned policy wins. Reinforce through culture that real-time courage is valued.

Professionals: Rehearse scenario-based ethics drills where tough, unexpected questions demand unscripted integrity.

♥ Building a Legacy Through Impromptu Influence

High-stakes leadership moments accumulate to shape legacy. The prepared speeches may be archived, but it is often the unscripted responses that endure in memory. Impromptu influence becomes the crucible in which reputations are forged.

The Enduring Impact

When historians, journalists, or employees recall leaders, they often cite unscripted moments: the quote at a crisis press conference, the rallying cry in adversity, the vulnerable admission of fault. These moments become shorthand for leadership identity. A leader's legacy is often measured not by their perfectly polished statements but by their ability to embody values authentically in the heat of the moment.

Research on memory suggests that people recall peak emotional moments more vividly than routine information. This means that a single Impromptu phrase can outweigh months of scripted communication. The credibility of leaders rests on how they handle these defining flashes of unscripted speech.

♥ Case Studies: Legacy Forged in Words

The Resigning Leader: A CEO, announcing resignation amid controversy, set tone by speaking directly, without notes: "I accept responsibility, and I believe the company will thrive beyond me." That unscripted line re-shaped his exit as honorable.

The Wartime Prime Minister: Known for fiery unscripted re-marks, his extemporaneous defiance inspired citizens far more than prepared addresses. His brief, off-the-cuff phrases— "We shall never surrender"— outlasted volumes of policy.

The Grassroots Activist: Without speechwriters or teleprompters, she improvised speeches that fueled movements remembered decades later. Her words live on in oral tradition, proving that legacies often grow from authenticity more than oratory.

Historical Example: John F. Kennedy's unscripted remarks in Ber-lin— "Ich bin ein Berliner"—became iconic, a defining statement of solidarity, though delivered spontaneously.

Corporate Pioneer: A founder, after selling his company, answered a last-minute question from employees: "The best legacy is not this company, but the courage you now have to build the next one." That Impromptu en-couragement seeded a culture of innovation.

♥ Cross-Domain Parallels

Legacy through Impromptu echoes natural law: rivers carve landscapes not through single floods but through repeated, unscripted flow over time. In science, it is similar to evolutionary adaptation—small adjustments creating lasting impact. In art, jazz legends like Miles Davis left their mark not through rehearsed notes but through improvisation that shaped entire genres. In na-ture, oak trees grow mighty not by sudden surges but by steady, consistent growth—each ring telling the story of enduring strength.

Practical Application

Leaders: Reflect after each high-stakes Impromptu moment on lessons for legacy. Journal these moments for self-awareness.

———— ✦ ——— ✦ ———ễ ễ ễễ ễ ễ———— ✦ ——— ✦ ———

"Silence filled with calm is interpreted as thoughtfulness, not weakness."

— Doctor Perspective™

Teams: Document powerful unscripted words for organizational culture. Share them in newsletters, reports, and rituals.

Organizations: Train leadership pipelines to see Impromptu not as accident but as opportunity for influence. Build resilience workshops that simulate legacy-defining moments.

Speakers-in-training: Study the unscripted remarks of historic figures to understand how authenticity crystallizes into legacy.

Conclusion:

High-stakes leadership moments strip communication to its core: clarity, empathy, courage, and adaptability. From crisis communication to ethical challenges, Impromptu speaking becomes the tool by which leader's steady storms, inspire hearts, negotiate peace, and forge legacy. Those who master this art not only navigate pressure but define eras.

JOURNAL
Write it Down Before It Escapes!

Chapter 14

Handling the Curveball Question with Grace

Look out for...

87) *Audiences judge leaders by how they respond when challenged.*

88) *An evasive or defensive answer erodes credibility.*

89) *A thoughtful, composed response, even if imperfect, builds trust.*

90) *Curveball questions resemble surprise weather in sailing. A skilled sailor doesn't curse the wind but adjusts the sails.*

91) *Not every curveball deserves a full swing.*

92) *The goal is not to dodge accountability but to steer toward clarity.*

93) *In sports, a batter can't predict every pitch but can train to adapt.*

The Unpredictable Nature of Curveball Questions

Every speaker eventually faces the dreaded curveball question: the unexpected inquiry that catches them off guard, threatens to derail their message, or exposes gaps in preparation. Curveball questions may come from journalists in a press conference, employees in a town hall, or panelists in a debate. What distinguishes great leaders and communicators is not the ability to avoid such questions but to handle them with composure, agility, and grace.

Why Curveballs Matter

Audiences often judge leaders not by their rehearsed remarks but by how they respond when challenged. An evasive or defensive answer erodes credibility. A thoughtful, composed response, even if imperfect, builds trust. Curveball questions reveal authenticity—whether leaders truly understand their subject, whether they can think on their feet, and whether they can communicate with honesty under pressure.

♥ Case Studies: The Curveball in Action

The Politician at a Town Hall: Asked a hostile question about corruption, she responded with transparency: "I understand why you ask that. Here are the steps we've taken, and here's what we're still improving." The candid, Impromptu reply softened critics.

The Scientist in a Media Interview: When asked an unrelated question about personal faith, he reframed gracefully: "That's important, but let me connect it to my work." He bridged the personal to the professional without alienating the audience.

The CEO at a Shareholder Meeting: Faced with an aggressive demand about salaries, he paused, acknowledged the frustration, and provided clear data before pivoting to the company's long-term vision. The composure under pressure calmed the room.

Cross-Domain Parallels

Curveball questions resemble surprise weather in sailing. A skilled sailor doesn't curse the wind but adjusts sails. In sports, a baseball batter cannot predict every pitch but can train to adapt swings. In nature, predators adapt instantly when prey zigzags. Flexibility is the universal key.

Practical Application

Speakers: Practice active listening—don't rush to answer before fully hearing the question.

Leaders: Learn bridging phrases ("What's essential here is...") to redirect hostile queries constructively.

Teams: Anticipate likely curveballs in advance so leaders can rehearse adaptive responses.

Professionals: Train under simulated hostile questioning to strengthen resilience.

♥ Techniques for Graceful Deflection

Not every curveball deserves a full swing. Sometimes the wisest response is a graceful deflection—addressing the spirit of the question without being trapped by its framing. The goal is not to dodge accountability but to steer toward clarity and constructive dialogue.

Methods of Deflection

Acknowledgment and Reframe: Validate the concern, then redirect. "That's a fair question. What's really at stake here is..." or, "That's a thoughtful question—I want to give it the clarity it deserves"

Pivot: Connect the question to your strength. "I haven't faced that exact situation, but here's what I've done in a similar context."

Partial Answer: Address what you can honestly, then pivot to broader context.

"Your first defense is composure."
— **Doctor Perspective™**

Humor: Used sparingly, humor can disarm hostility and reset tone.

Data Anchor: Use verifiable facts as stabilizers when emotions run high.

Practice Drill

With a partner or coach, collect 10 "curveball" questions—personal, professional, even absurd. Answer each in 30 seconds, focusing on the *acknowledge-reframe-pivot* cycle. Over time, the jolt of surprise diminishes, and composure becomes your default.

Case Studies

Media Example: A CEO facing hostile press about declining stock reframed: "Yes, the stock is down, but let's look at our five-year innovation pipeline." He acknowledged reality but shifted perspective.

Political Debate: A candidate asked about a personal misstep said with humor, "That was a mistake, and my spouse reminds me daily." The levity won the audience before he pivoted to policy.

Classroom Setting: A professor challenged by a provocative question responded: "I see why you ask. Let's explore the deeper issue behind it." She diffused conflict and enriched learning.

♥ Cross-Domain Parallels

Deflecting with grace is like aikido in martial arts: redirecting energy rather than resisting it head-on. In science, mirrors reflect light without absorbing heat—leaders can reflect hostility without letting it burn them.

Practical Application

Leaders: Prepare bridging statements that pivot toward vision.

Teams: Role-play hostile questions to strengthen leaders' agility.

Professionals: Balance honesty with diplomacy—never fabricate under pressure.

♥ Transforming Hostility into Opportunity

Curveball questions often come from skeptics or critics. Yet these moments also offer opportunities: a chance to demonstrate empathy, to reframe negativity, and to win over doubters. The most memorable communicators turn hostility into turning points.

Case Studies

Public Forum: A mayor, confronted angrily about taxes, began by empathizing: "I pay those taxes too." She then outlined reforms underway. The critic softened, and the crowd applauded.

Corporate Setting: A manager questioned aggressively about layoffs acknowledged pain, then used the moment to reaffirm the company's long-term stability. Employees later said that was the first time they trusted him.

Historical Example: Nelson Mandela, asked hostile questions after release from prison, responded with dignity: "I have no bitterness." His grace transformed suspicion into admiration.

♥ Cross-Domain Parallels

Turning hostility into opportunity is like composting waste into fertile soil. What seems destructive can become productive when reframed. In sports, consider basketball players converting fouls into free throws: pain becomes points. In nature, volcanoes destroy but also enrich soil for future harvests.

Practical Application

Leaders: Always acknowledge the emotion behind the question before addressing facts.

Speakers: Reframe critique as evidence of engagement: "I'm glad you asked because it shows you care."

Organizations: Train staff in de-escalation language that turns heat into dialogue.

✼✼✼✼✼✼✼✼✼✼— ♣ — ♣ —✼✼✼✼✼✼✼✼✼✼

"No word was ever as effective as a rightly timed pause."
— **Mark Twain**

♥ Building Mental Agility for the Unexpected

Handling curveball questions with grace is not accidental; it is the result of cultivated mental agility. Leaders must train their minds to remain calm under pressure, to see patterns in chaos, and to respond creatively in the moment.

♥ Methods for Building Agility

Scenario Drills: Simulate high-pressure questioning with minimal PREP time.

Mindfulness: Practice mental stillness to reduce panic reflex.

Framework Familiarity: Know structures like PREP (Point, Reason, Example, Point) that provide fallback order.

Cross-Training: Engage in improvisational theater, debate, or rapid problem-solving games.

Case Studies

Corporate Leadership Program: Executives drilled in surprise Q&A learned to frame answers clearly in under 30 seconds.

Military Training: Officers practiced Impromptu debriefs under stress, building resilience for battlefield communication.

Science Outreach: Scientists in media bootcamps learned to answer unpredictable questions by translating jargon into metaphors.

♥ Cross-Domain Parallels

Mental agility is like a gymnast's flexibility—practiced through repeti-

~~~~~~~~~~~~~ •••••••• ~~~~~~~~~~~~~
"Audiences are quick to judge. Influence their verdict."
— **Doctor Perspective™**

tion until instinctive. In nature, think of octopuses adapting instantly to camouflage in new environments. In technology, algorithms adjust in milliseconds to shifting data inputs. Humans, too, can train adaptability.

Practical Application

Leaders: Build "response muscles" through repeated unscripted practice.

Teams: Encourage environments where candid questions are welcomed, not feared.

Professionals: Treat every curveball as training for the next one—growth through exposure.

Conclusion:

Curveball questions are inevitable in leadership and communication. What sets apart effective leaders is not avoidance but agility. By listening deeply, deflecting with grace, reframing hostility, and building mental flexibility, speakers transform disruptive questions into defining moments of trust and influence.

※※※※※※※※※※— ♣ — ♣ —※※※※※※※※※※

Whatever is true, whatever is noble, whatever is right, whatever is pure, whatever is lovely, whatever is admirable—if anything is excellent or praiseworthy—think about such things.

Philippians 4:8

JOURNAL
Write it Down Before It Escapes!

Chapter 15

When the Mind Goes Blank: Recovery Strategies That Work

Look out for...

94) *Blankness resembles a computer buffering: the system is still working, just catching up.*

95) *In jazz, silence between notes is as meaningful as the notes themselves.*

96) *In rhetoric, repetition is a respected device—it reinforces meaning while camouflaging hesitation.*

97) *Quick recovery is like martial arts: when knocked off balance, fighters roll and stand.*

98) *Triage nurses prioritize under pressure: imperfect but immediate action is better than paralysis.*

99) *Cognitive-behavioral research shows that shifting self-talk changes performance.*

100) *Mindset shifts are like weather fronts—storms dissipate when pressure drops.*

♥ The Fear of Blankness

One of the greatest fears in public speaking is going blank. The words vanish, the mind freezes, and silence stretches longer with each passing second. This moment terrifies beginners and unnerves seasoned professionals alike. But blankness is not the end of a speech—it is an opportunity to demonstrate resilience, adaptability, and even humor.

♥ Why Blankness Happens

Blankness is often triggered by stress, fatigue, or sudden distraction. The brain's working memory overloads, leaving the speaker momentarily speechless. Neuroscience shows that cortisol spikes under pressure can inhibit retrieval of stored information. Yet the audience often perceives blank moments less harshly than speakers imagine; what matters is how recovery is handled.

Blankness also arises from over-reliance on memorization. When a speaker depends entirely on rote recall, a single disruption can unravel the sequence. By contrast, those who anchor ideas in structures, stories, or frameworks recover more easily. Stress inoculation theory in psychology suggests that exposing oneself to small "failures" in practice—like intentional pauses or planted distractions—reduces the fear of blankness in live scenarios.

Case Studies

Conference Speaker: In the middle of a keynote, a consultant forgot his next point. He smiled, took a sip of water, and said, "I just gave you a live demo of why pauses matter." The audience laughed, and he regained rhythm.

Debate Stage: A student froze during a competition. Instead of panicking, she repeated the last phrase slowly, giving her mind time to reset. Judges later praised her composure.

~~~~~~~~~~~~~~ ●●●●●●●● ~~~~~~~~~~~~~~

"One sentence is often enough. Two may be too many!"

— **Doctor Perspective**™

Political Rally: A candidate blanked on statistics but pivoted with a personal story. The anecdote connected emotionally, overshadowing the forgotten data.

Historical Example: Winston Churchill, once mocked for pausing too long, reframed the silence as gravitas. What began as a lapse became a hallmark of power.

Corporate Training: A manager froze during a presentation but admitted, "I blanked—let me reset." The candor earned empathy and respect from her team.

♥ Cross-Domain Parallels

Blankness resembles a computer buffering: the system is still working, just catching up. In sports, athletes sometimes "choke" under pressure but recover by resetting focus. In nature, deer freeze briefly when startled, then resume motion. The pause itself is not failure—it is part of the cycle. In jazz, silence between notes is as meaningful as the notes themselves. Likewise, pauses in speaking can be reinterpreted as intentional beats of reflection rather than signs of collapse.

Practical Application

Speakers: Normalize blankness as a temporary pause, not catastrophe.

Leaders: Use humor or transparency to reset without embarrassment.

Teams: Support colleagues in group presentations with seamless handoffs.

Professionals: Practice recovery drills by intentionally stopping mid-speech and resuming.

Trainers: Encourage deliberate blank simulations so learners embrace, not fear, silence.

♥ Techniques for Quick Recovery

The difference between disaster and triumph lies in recovery. Blankness can last seconds or ruin minutes, depending on strategy. Effective speakers cultivate recovery techniques until they become instinctive.

Recovery Methods

Pause and Breathe: When blankness strikes, the most powerful first move is to pause and breathe. Instead of panicking, inhaling slowly through the nose and exhaling through the mouth calms the nervous system, lowering cortisol levels. This physiological reset clears pathways for memory retrieval. A deliberate pause also communicates confidence to the audience, signaling that silence is intentional, not a collapse. Many skilled speakers train themselves to count three deep breaths when blankness hits. This not only buys time but also resets rhythm, allowing thoughts to flow again.

Repeat Last Line: Repetition acts as both a bridge and a lifeline. By restating the last complete sentence or phrase, speakers create continuity for the audience while giving their brain a chance to retrieve the next idea. For example, if a presenter said, "Our greatest challenge is..." and blanks, repeating that phrase gives the mind a second chance to complete the thought. Audiences perceive it as emphasis, not failure. In rhetoric, repetition is a respected device—it reinforces meaning while camouflaging hesitation.

Summarize So Far: A practical way to regain control is to recap what has been covered. By summarizing key points— "So far, we've looked at the challenge, the options, and the opportunity"—the speaker not only resets their own mental map but also strengthens the audience's retention. Summaries create clarity and often trigger recall of what comes next. Listeners appreciate the reinforcement, making the technique doubly effective.

Bridge Technique: The bridge technique involves pivoting from the blank to a pre-prepared anecdote, story, or example. Instead of forcing recall, the speaker smoothly says, "This reminds me of..." and moves into familiar territory. From there, they can circle back to the forgotten point. This tactic

"Suit the action to the word, the word to the action."
— **William Shakespeare**

creates the impression of intentional redirection. Skilled communicators build a small library of "bridge stories" ready for such moments.

Audience Engagement: Turning to the audience is a powerful recovery method. Asking a rhetorical question like "How many of you have faced this?" or inviting quick input creates interaction while buying time. Engagement flips the pressure, shifting focus from the speaker to the audience. When the speaker resumes, the connection feels stronger, and the blankness is often forgotten.

Humor as Reset: Humor diffuses tension instantly. A speaker who laughs at their own blankness communicates humanity and relatability. For instance, saying, "I had a brilliant point here, but apparently it was too brilliant to stay in my head," draws laughter and resets the atmosphere. The danger is overuse—humor must feel authentic, not defensive. Used wisely, it transforms failure into shared amusement and demonstrates composure under pressure.

Case Studies

CEO Town Hall: Forgetting the next slide, the CEO asked employees, "What's the biggest challenge you see daily?" The pause became dialogue, and the meeting thrived.

Teacher in Classroom: Lost track mid-lecture, she said, "Let's recap together." Students contributed, helping her reset.

Stand-Up Comic: Went blank but improvised: "That joke was so bad, my brain refused to deliver it." The humor won cheers.

Media Interview: A spokesperson froze under tough questioning but repeated the last key phrase: "Our commitment is clear—our commitment is..." and then regained flow. The audience saw determination, not failure.

Sports Coaching: A coach blanked in a timeout huddle, then asked players, "What are you seeing?" The collaborative moment galvanized the team.

♥ Cross-Domain Parallels

Quick recovery is like martial arts: when knocked off balance, fighters roll and stand. In music, jazz musicians cover mistakes by improvising riffs. In technology, autopilot systems take over briefly until pilots regain control. In medicine, triage nurses prioritize under pressure: imperfect but immediate action is better than paralysis.

Practical Application

Speakers: Train on-the-spot fillers that buy thinking time.

Teams: Encourage shared recovery signals in group presentations.

Organizations: Include recovery scenarios in public speaking workshops.

Coaches: Frame mistakes as training material, not shame.

♥ Mindset Shifts: From Panic to Poise

The blank moment feels catastrophic, but mindset reframing transforms it into an ordinary, manageable event.

The Psychological Battle

Blankness often escalates because of self-criticism: "I'm failing." The inner critic takes over, amplifying fear and making recovery harder. This spiral is familiar to anyone who has panicked in front of an audience. Speakers imagine judgmental thoughts from listeners— "They think I'm incompetent"— when in reality, most audiences empathize. By recognizing this cognitive distortion, speakers can break the cycle.

Reframing is critical. Cognitive-behavioral research shows that shifting self-talk changes performance. Instead of "I'm failing," a speaker can think, "This pause gives me power." Elite athletes use similar reframing to manage high-stakes pressure, interpreting nerves as readiness rather than weakness. The same works for speakers: labeling silence as composure alters perception.

Blankness is also intensified by perfectionism. Leaders who demand flawless delivery crumble when disrupted. Accepting imperfection liberates the mind. Barack Obama, in early campaign speeches, reframed pauses as reflection, signaling thoughtfulness. This mindset shift transforms what feels like collapse into presence.

Transition: Winning this inner contest is not only about reframing thoughts—it is also about having a practical game plan in the moment. When the mind screams "panic," structure restores control. That is where the *90-Second Survival Blueprint* comes in: a clear, step-by-step method to channel nervous energy into a confident response.

♥ The 90-Second Survival Blueprint

When you blank out or stumble mid-speech, the clock feels like your enemy. In reality, you have more time than you think. Ninety seconds—about the length of a deep breath and a short paragraph—can reset your rhythm, recover your composure, and even turn the moment into one of strength.

Pause (0–10 seconds): Stop talking. Breathe. Plant your feet. Own the silence instead of fleeing from it. A calm pause communicates authority far more than frantic filler words.

Reframe (10–30 seconds): Convert panic into a narrative. Say aloud, "Let me approach that from another angle," or "That's a powerful question." This buys time and signals thoughtfulness.

Rebuild (30–60 seconds): Deliver a short, structured point you *do* know—use a story, analogy, or fact from your toolbox. This re-anchors your credibility.

Redirect (60–90 seconds): Land on a clear conclusion, even if brief. "Here's the key takeaway..." or "If you remember only one thing, it's this..." End with control rather than drift.

Handled with intention, those ninety seconds don't expose your weakness—they highlight your resilience. The audience remembers not the

✳✳✳✳✳✳✳✳✳✳— ♣— ♣—✳✳✳✳✳✳✳✳✳✳

"An evasive or defensive answer erodes credibility."

— Doctor Perspective™

stumble, but the recovery.

Case Studies

Medical Conference: A doctor blanked on terminology but reframed aloud: "I could give you the Latin, but here's the plain-English version." The audience applauded the clarity.

Boardroom Pitch: An entrepreneur lost her place but said, "This silence is me making sure I get this right." Investors admired her honesty.

Church Sermon: A pastor paused mid-sermon, prayed quietly, then resumed stronger. Congregants described it as powerful authenticity.

Historic Example: Barack Obama, in early campaign speeches, sometimes paused when blanking on phrasing. By calmly reframing pauses as moments of reflection, he built an image of thoughtful leadership.

Athletics Parallel: Gymnasts who stumble in routines are trained to smile and continue, reframing errors as part of the show. Speakers can adopt the same mindset.

♥ Cross-Domain Parallels

Mindset shifts are like weather fronts—storms dissipate when pressure drops. In sports, tennis players reframe errors as learning points mid-match. In biology, stress-adapted plants thrive after drought because their systems normalize pressure. In aviation, pilots describe "the pause" as recalibration, not failure. In art, negative space brings balance to composition; in speech, pauses can do the same.

Practical Application

Leaders: Practice self-talk like "This pause is power."

Speakers: Reframe blankness as audience engagement space.

※※※※※※※※※※— ♣ — ♣ —※※※※※※※※※※

"I have made this letter longer only because I had not the leisure to make it shorter."

— **Blaise Pascal**

Professionals: Integrate mindfulness to reduce fear of silence.

Teams: Debrief blank moments as learning opportunities, not shameful lapses.

♥ Preparing for the Inevitable

Blankness is not preventable, but it can be anticipated. The most resilient communicators prepare strategies knowing blanks will come.

Preparation Tactics

Fallback Frameworks: Frameworks like PREP (Point, Reason, Example, Point) or the rule-of-three provide mental scaffolding. When recall falters, the speaker can rely on these skeletons to rebuild thought flow. For instance, if forgetting details in a business pitch, returning to the PREP structure helps organize: "Here's the point, here's why it matters, here's an example, and here's the reinforcement." Practicing frameworks until instinctive ensures they emerge under pressure.

Story Library: A repertoire of short, versatile stories functions as a rescue kit. If memory collapses, pivoting to a story keeps the audience engaged while allowing recall to catch up. Stories connect emotionally, so even if the exact point is delayed, the audience remains captivated. Speakers should categorize stories into themes—resilience, teamwork, innovation—so one fits any moment.

Memory Cues: Small prompts—keywords on notecards, images on slides, or even objects on stage—act as anchors. These cues spark recall and prevent total derailment. For example, a slide with a single word ("Trust") can remind the speaker of an entire section. Effective speakers rehearse with these cues, ensuring familiarity.

Recovery Practice: Just as athletes scrimmage to simulate fatigue, speakers should drill intentional blanks. Practicing recovery builds confidence. One exercise is to stop mid-sentence during rehearsal and force a

~~~~~~~~~~~~~~ ••••••• ~~~~~~~~~~~~~~
"Give every man thy ear, but few thy voice."
— **William Shakespeare**

pivot. Over time, this inoculates the brain against panic. Toastmasters' clubs often integrate Table Topics for this reason—training spontaneous recall under observation.

Peer Support Systems: In group presentations, colleagues can be lifelines. Establishing cues—like subtle gestures or phrases—enables teammates to step in seamlessly. For example, one speaker might say, "I'll let my colleague expand," allowing another to cover. This not only rescues the blanked speaker but demonstrates teamwork.

Case Studies

Executive Retreat: Leaders practiced intentional blanks. One remarked, "I realized the audience isn't hostile—they're patient."

University Speech Class: Students drilled recovery phrases, reporting greater confidence in competitions.

Media Interview: A spokesperson admitted, "Let me clarify," then delivered a rehearsed fallback. The audience never noticed.

Conference Panel: A panelist forgot her argument but used a backup story, which ended up being the highlight of the discussion.

Sports Setting: A player giving post-game remarks froze, then used humor: "I forgot my line, but we remembered how to win." The authenticity drew cheers.

♥ Cross-Domain Parallels

Preparing for blanks is like carrying spare tires on a road trip. In aviation, pilots train for engine stalls so recovery becomes automatic. In nature, squirrels hide food caches for winter scarcity. In theater, understudies rehearse entire plays not expecting to perform, but ready when needed. Preparation does not prevent the blank but ensures the show goes on.

Practical Application

Leaders: Build blank-proof habits with fallback stories.

Teams: Practice group rescues for colleagues.

Organizations: Normalize training with intentional silence drills.

Individuals: Keep a personal toolkit of metaphors or stories as safety nets.

Conclusion

Blank moments are inevitable. What matters is how speakers recover—with poise, humor, or adaptive strategy. By normalizing blankness, rehearsing recovery, and reframing it as part of communication, leaders turn fear into credibility. Grace under silence often speaks louder than words. The best communicators transform blankness into brilliance, proving that resilience under pressure is the true measure of mastery.

JOURNAL
Write it Down Before It Escapes!

◇◆◇◆◇— ♣— ♣—◇◆◇◆◇— ♣— ♣—◇◆◇◆◇

"Energy matters... not just content."
— **Doctor Perspective™**

◇ ♦ ◇ ♦ ◇— ♣ — ♣ —◇ ♦ ◇ ♦ ◇— ♣ — ♣ —◇ ♦ ◇ ♦ ◇

Whatever is true, whatever is noble, whatever is right, whatever is pure, whatever is lovely, whatever is admirable—if anything is excellent or praiseworthy—think about such things.

Philippians 4:8

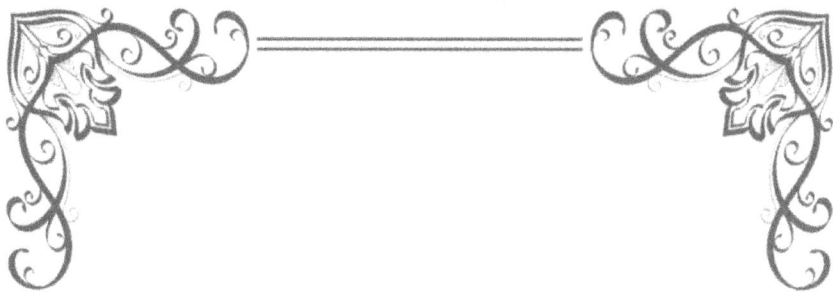

Chapter 16

"Impromptu Speech Takeover: Communication Domination"

Look out for...

101) Silence filled with calm is interpreted as thoughtfulness, not weakness.

102) In professional settings, confidence is often judged in the first seconds.

103) Smiling conveys openness and warmth, creating rapport before the first word is spoken.

104) The question is your foundation.

105) In Impromptu speaking, the first breath is the first victory.

106) A missed nuance in the question leads to a misplaced response.

107) Brevity signals clarity and respect.

108) The question is your foundation. Do not segue!

You've learned the building blocks: how to manage fear, sharpen mental reflexes, build a toolbox of stories, craft powerful openings, harness humor, and command voice and body. But skills in isolation aren't enough. Real mastery is measured in the moment, under pressure, when you have no script and no safety net.

This chapter brings everything together into a single countdown system—a structured drill tested in Impromptu Speech Clubs and transferable to the workplace. Think of it as your practicum: the arena where you pull every tool into play.

♥ The Anatomy of an Impromptu Speech

Every effective Impromptu speech has a recognizable structure. It may last just one or two minutes, but those moments can be organized into a miniature speech with a beginning, middle, and end. Understanding the anatomy of an Impromptu speech equips the speaker to maximize impact within very limited time.

Opening (15 seconds)

The opening must establish presence instantly. Instead of repeating the question verbatim, a strong opening reframes or acknowledges it with a fresh perspective. This captures attention, sets tone, and signals confidence. A pause, a smile, or a brief anecdote can buy seconds while shaping the first impression.

Body (60–90 seconds)

The body carries the weight of the message. Here, the speaker uses a model to organize ideas quickly. Common approaches include:

The W's (Who, What, Where, When, Why, How): A natural way to break down a topic.

Chronology: Past–Present–Future or Before–During–After.

Pros and Cons: Balanced analysis leading to a conclusion.

Argument Models: State a position, support with evidence, address counterpoints.

Personal Story: Ground abstract questions in concrete experience.

Any of these can turn a random prompt into a coherent, audience-friendly message.

Conclusion (20–30 seconds)

The conclusion should avoid trailing off. Instead, it must land firmly with a call-to-action, a clear takeaway, or an insight for the audience. The goal is not to summarize the entire body but to crystallize one central message. The last words should make the speech sound intentional, complete, and memorable.

Why Anatomy Matters

When speakers internalize this structure—Opening, Body, Conclusion—they stop fearing the unknown. Whatever the question, they know where to start, how to build, and when to finish. It is not about filling every second, but about filling every second with purpose.

Countdown to Domination – In the Club or Contest

In the Impromptu Speech Club or contest environment, success depends not on chance but on disciplined process. Over the years, a tested, step-by-step method has emerged that helps speakers remain calm, think clearly, and deliver with impact. These progressive steps form a mental and physical checklist that turns chaos into confidence.

◊ ♦ ◊ ♦ ◊— ♣ — ♣ —◊ ♦ ◊ ♦ ◊— ♣ — ♣ —◊ ♦ ◊ ♦ ◊

"The question is your foundation."
— Doctor Perspective™

Step 1 – Breathe Deeply

Before words come, air must flow. A deep breath calms nerves, slows the racing heart, and signals to the body that control has been regained. In Impromptu speaking, the first breath is the first victory.

Step 2 – Display Confidence

Even before speaking, posture and demeanor communicate authority. Stand tall, shoulders back, and eyes lifted. Confidence displayed externally often generates confidence internally.

Step 3 – Smile

A simple smile disarms both fear and the audience. Smiling conveys openness and warmth, creating rapport before the first word is spoken.

Step 4 – Posture and Presence

Step into position with intention. Plant feet firmly, balanced, and poised. Avoid shifting nervously. A stable stance anchors thought and speech alike.

Step 5 – Distance Yourself from Past and Future

Do not dwell on mistakes made earlier in the meeting, nor fear judgments that may come later. The only reality that matters is the present moment—the question at hand.

Step 6 – Listen Carefully

The question is your foundation. Listen fully, resisting the urge to rehearse an answer prematurely. A missed nuance in the question leads to a misplaced response.

Step 7 – Identify the Trigger Word or Idea

Every Impromptu question has a trigger—one word or phrase that unlocks a direction. Grasp it quickly, and clarity follows.

Step 8 – Take the Unusual Approach

Avoid the obvious, which leads to clichés. A fresh angle or unexpected story not only impresses judges but also delights audiences.

Step 9 – Use Economy of Words

With time limited, every sentence must earn its place. Concise phrasing demonstrates clarity of thought and respect for the listener's attention.

Step 10 – Manage Time with the Lights

In contests or club practice, speakers use timing lights: green (begin), yellow (transition), red (conclude). Skilled speakers pace their content to land powerfully at the red, not stumble past it.

Step 11 – Finish with a Call-to-Action

Do not drift off. Conclude with a clear takeaway, challenge, or encouragement for the audience. The call-to-action transforms a brief answer into a lasting impact.

♥ **Countdown to Domination – At the Workplace & Beyond**

The very same steps that guide a speaker through an Impromptu Speech Club question can be applied directly to the workplace. Meetings, interviews, crisis briefings, and chance encounters all demand clear thinking on the spot. By translating the Club method into professional contexts, the Impromptu discipline becomes a career asset.

Step 1 – Breathe Deeply

When a tough question comes in a meeting or interview, pause for one deliberate breath. Silence filled with calm is interpreted as thoughtfulness, not weakness.

Step 2 – Display Confidence

In professional settings, confidence is often judged in the first second. Sit upright or stand tall, make eye contact, and let your presence project competence.

Step 3 – Smile

Even in tense boardrooms, a genuine smile disarms hostility and shows composure. A smile says, "I'm not rattled; I'm ready."

Step 4 – Posture and Presence

Avoid fidgeting or defensive gestures (crossed arms, tapping pens). Grounded posture communicates steadiness under pressure.

Step 5 – Focus on the Present

Leave behind the fear of past mistakes or future consequences. Answer the question asked—here and now. Professionals earn trust by being fully present.

Step 6 – Listen Carefully

Executives, clients, and colleagues all notice whether their words are heard. Listening fully prevents embarrassment and ensures answers fit the true question.

Step 7 – Identify the Trigger Word or Idea

In workplace questions, the "trigger" may be a term like *budget, deadline,* or *morale.* Seizing on that keyword provides a natural starting point.

Step 8 – Take the Unusual Approach

In business, fresh perspectives differentiate. Instead of repeating clichés, tell a brief story, cite an unexpected analogy, or connect to values that matter.

Step 9 – Use Economy of Words

Meetings reward conciseness. A sharp, two-minute contribution often outweighs a rambling ten-minute monologue. Brevity signals clarity and respect.

Step 10 – Manage Time Intentionally

Even without lights, time awareness is crucial. In interviews or panels, aim for structured, concise answers that leave space for follow-up questions.

Step 11 – End with a Call-to-Action or Takeaway

In workplace responses, close with a practical suggestion, affirmation, or invitation: *"Here's how we can move forward."* That final push leaves the impression of leadership.

♥ **Styles of Impromptu Speech Questions**

Not all Impromptu questions are created equal. The style of the question shapes the style of the response. Skilled speakers recognize the type quickly and adapt their structure accordingly. For the Impromptu Speech Club, contests, or professional environments, these are the most common categories:

Single-Word Question

A single word (*"Hope"* ... *"Technology"* ... *"Failure"*) demands that the speaker frame meaning from scratch. This style tests creativity and quick association.

Relay Question

The next speaker is asked to build on the previous one. This requires listening, flexibility, and the ability to transition smoothly. It mirrors real-world scenarios where professionals must contribute to ongoing discussions without repeating others.

Controversial Question

These questions deliberately touch on sensitive or debatable issues. They test composure, diplomacy, and balance. The goal is not necessarily to take sides, but to frame a thoughtful, audience-respectful position.

Argumentative Question

A step further than controversial, these questions push the speaker to defend or refute a position directly. Handling them well demonstrates logic and persuasion under pressure.

"Let every person be quick to hear, slow to speak, slow to anger."
— James 1:19

Absurdity Question

Designed to test imagination, absurd prompts (*"If cats ruled the world..."*) measure a speaker's creativity, humor, and flexibility. Done well, absurd answers can be highly entertaining while still structured.

Truncated Question

Questions cut off mid-thought force the speaker to finish and interpret creatively. They simulate real interruptions or half-formed queries in life, demanding composure and initiative.

Recognizing these types allows speakers to adjust instantly—choosing a framework, tone, and style appropriate to the challenge. What seems random is, in fact, a patterned opportunity.

♥ The Role of the Impromptu Speech Question Master

No Impromptu session succeeds without a capable guide. The Impromptu Speech Question Master is not a filler role, but the architect of the experience. Their task is to craft questions that challenge, inspire, and stretch participants while ensuring fairness and flow.

Impromptu Speech training best-practices dictate that before any session begins at the Club or training level, there must be a clear statement of the objectives of the session. It can be focusing on a tight "Opening, Body and Conclusion". It could be "Transitions". It could be the "Interweaving of Humor". It could be a "Dynamic Call to Action". It could be "Effective Use of Speech Title". It could be "Creative Openings & Climactic Endings". Whatever it is, there must have been training provided, either during the session or on a previous occasion. The rule is Teach and Train before your Test.

Minimum Experience

A Question Master should never be someone avoiding participation. To lead others effectively, they must have answered at least six Impromptu ques-

"After you know what you want to say, the only task left is practice."
— **Doctor Perspective™**

tions themselves. Credibility comes from lived experience, not theory.

Knowing the Audience

Effective Question Masters consider the age, culture, and experience of the group. A question that inspires seasoned leaders may overwhelm a newcomer. The Master adapts prompts so that everyone feels stretched but not paralyzed.

Crafting the Questions

Variety is key. Questions should include different styles—single-word, relay, absurdity, controversial—so that participants learn to adapt in diverse ways. The goal is not to stump speakers, but to bring out their best thinking.

Encouraging Best Practice

The Master reminds participants of fundamentals: breathe, pause, and conclude with purpose. Gentle reminders before a session keep the discipline alive.

Guarding Against Segues

Some speakers attempt to dodge the question with unrelated stories. The Question Master should encourage participants to stay on point while still allowing creativity. Relevance trains discipline.

Time Management

Sessions are not endless. The Question Master keeps answers within the agreed timing (often 1–2 minutes), ensuring fairness and energy throughout.

Evaluation Role

Feedback must be either instant, or as close to the conclusion of the speech as possible. should be concise—30 to 45 seconds at most. The goal is to highlight one strength and one growth area. Lengthy evaluations drain energy from the session; sharp, constructive comments fuel growth.

The Evaluator role does not have to be restricted to the Question Master, and can be assigned to another Club member who has excelled at Impromptu Speaking. The advantage to this approach is that the Evaluator gets to hear both the question and the response, and both objectively.

On the other hand, the Question Master, having crafted the question with an objective in mind, has the advantage in determining whether or not the objective has been met.

The Impromptu Speech Question Master embodies the principle: ***practice with purpose.*** When guided well, an Impromptu session transforms from a random exercise into a masterclass of growth.

Having mastered the mechanics of Impromptu speaking through structured steps and practical frameworks, the next challenge is learning to connect with audiences in a way that makes them lean in, relax, and trust you. That bridge is humor—not as a gimmick, but as a strategic tool for influence.

♥ Final Countdown

If you take nothing else from this book, take this countdown. It is the blueprint for domination—practiced in contests, proven in classrooms, validated in boardrooms. Every time you face a surprise question, remember: anchor yourself, move with clarity, land with impact.

Domination is not about perfection. It is about presence. And with this countdown, presence is always within your reach.

◇ ♦ ◇ ♦ ◇— ♣ — ♣ —◇ ♦ ◇ ♦ ◇— ♣ — ♣ —◇ ♦ ◇ ♦ ◇

*"**Real** humility requires having value to offer, and effectively delivering it with clarity and sincerity"*

— **Doctor Perspective™**

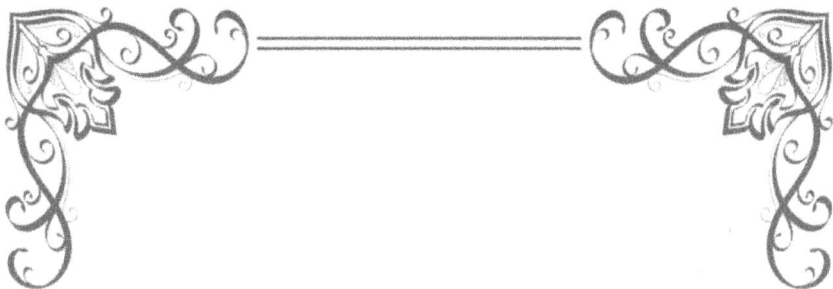

Chapter 17

Stand Out and Spark Smiles

Look out for...

109) Humor succeeds not only because of what is said but how and when it is delivered.

110) A well-timed pause is the secret sauce of humor.

111) Pausing before the punchline builds anticipation.

112) In professional environments, humor works best when it builds unity, not when it undermines seriousness.

113) Smiles are a subtle yet powerful form of agreement.

114) Aim to spark smiles as your baseline; laughter is a bonus.

115) Humor, used wisely, is one of the most potent connectors in communication.

116) Humor without timing, tone, and tact is like music without rhythm: noise instead of harmony.

♥ The Power of Humor in Impromptu Speaking

Humor, used wisely, is one of the most potent connectors in communication. It relaxes tension, opens minds, and makes a speaker unforgettable. In Impromptu settings, where nerves run high and uncertainty looms, the ability to spark genuine smiles can transform the entire experience for both speaker and audience.

Why Humor Works

Humor taps into biology as much as psychology. Laughter triggers the release of endorphins—natural chemicals that reduce stress and increase bonding. Social scientists have shown that groups who laugh together trust each other more. Neuroscience adds another dimension: mirror neurons fire when we see someone else smile or laugh, priming us to do the same. This explains why even a subtle, shared chuckle can shift the energy of a room.

♥ Humor as Memory Glue

Research consistently shows that people remember information tied to humor more than facts delivered plainly. A well-placed quip can anchor your message long after details fade. This is especially valuable in Impromptu speaking, where clarity and memorability must be achieved quickly.

Case Studies

Club Contest: A nervous member faced the question, "What is your greatest weakness?" She grinned and answered, "Chocolate—because I've never been able to resist it." The room laughed, and she flowed naturally into a deeper reflection on self-control.

Professional Setting: In a tense budget meeting, an executive began, "I know finance isn't everyone's favorite topic, but I promise no math test at the end." The humor broke the ice and paved the way for collaboration.

"All the great speakers were bad speakers at first."

— **Ralph Waldo Emerson**

Historical Example: Ronald Reagan, questioned about his age in a debate, quipped, "I won't exploit my opponent's youth and inexperience." The line not only neutralized criticism but won hearts nationwide.

♥ The Danger of Misused Humor

Not all humor helps. Misjudged attempts can alienate, offend, or trivialize. In Impromptu speaking, where there's no rehearsal, humor must be light, respectful, and inclusive. Sarcasm or humor at someone else's expense nearly always backfires.

Timing, Tone, and Tact

Humor succeeds not only because of *what* is said but *how* and *when* it is delivered. A simple phrase can become hilarious—or fall flat—depending on timing, tone, and tact. In Impromptu speaking, where there is no rehearsal, these three elements become the difference between connection and misfire.

Timing

A well-timed pause is the secret sauce of humor. Pausing just before the punchline builds anticipation. Pausing just after gives space for laughter to land. Without that space, humor evaporates. Experienced speakers learn to "read the room," holding silence for a heartbeat longer than feels natural to let anticipation grow. In Impromptu moments, silence becomes a powerful ally.

Tone

Tone shapes intent. A warm, playful tone signals friendliness; a sharp, sarcastic tone risks sounding cruel. Audiences forgive clumsy phrasing if the tone is kind, but even clever words fall flat if the tone feels hostile. The safest rule: deliver humor as if you were laughing with, never at, your audience.

Tact

Tact protects the speaker from turning humor into harm. Every audience has cultural, generational, and personal sensitivities. What earns a laugh in one setting can wound in another. For example, joking about workplace stress might win smiles among peers but appear dismissive to a burned-out

Case Studies

Boardroom Misstep: A CEO joked, "We don't need vacations; we live here at the office." Instead of laughter, weary employees felt resentment. Timing and tact were both missing.

Successful Classroom Example: A teacher, introducing a difficult subject, said, "Don't worry—this won't be on the test. Actually, there is no test." The room filled with laughter and relief, making space for learning.

Practical Application

Pause before and after key lines to maximize impact.

Match tone with your intent: playful, not biting.

Check tact by asking yourself: Could this hurt, exclude, or embarrass?

Humor without timing, tone, and tact is like music without rhythm: noise instead of harmony.

♥ Humor Across Contexts

Humor is not one-size-fits-all. The kind of humor that works in a relaxed gathering can feel wildly out of place in a boardroom or courtroom. The skilled Impromptu speaker learns to adapt humor to the setting, making it appropriate, relevant, and effective across contexts.

Humor in the Workplace

In professional environments, humor works best when it builds unity, not when it undermines seriousness. A light remark about shared frustrations—like a perpetually jammed printer—creates bonding without

◇ ♦ ◇ ♦ ◇— ♣ — ♣ —◇ ♦ ◇ ♦ ◇— ♣ — ♣ —◇ ♦ ◇ ♦ ◇

"Flexibility is the universal key that unlocks many seemingly impenetrable opportunities."

— Doctor Perspective™

trivializing the work. In tense meetings, humor that acknowledges the pressure while offering relief shows emotional intelligence.

Humor in Public Speaking

In speeches, humor should serve the message, not overshadow it. A brief anecdote or witty remark at the start can win attention, but the speaker must transition seamlessly into substance. Overloading a talk with humor risks leaving audiences entertained but unchanged. The balance is to use humor as seasoning, not the main dish.

Humor in Interpersonal Situations

Even one-on-one, humor is powerful. Leaders who share a laugh with colleagues signal approachability and humility. In conflict situations, humor can defuse tension and open the door for dialogue.

Case Studies

Workplace Example: A project manager facing missed deadlines quipped, "We've just discovered a new unit of time: the project week—it lasts 14 days." The humor softened frustration and restored morale.

Public Speech: A civic leader opening a talk on taxes said, "I know what you're thinking: don't quit your day job. That's why I'm here—to talk about jobs." The wordplay sparked grins, leading smoothly into serious content.

Interpersonal: A doctor calming a nervous patient said, "Don't worry, I've done this once before—today." The humor lightened the mood while reinforcing competence.

Practical Applications

In the workplace: keep humor light and collective.

On stage: let humor serve, not steal, the message.

One-on-one: use humor to lower barriers and humanize yourself.

Humor that adapts to the context is never accidental; it is the result of observation, sensitivity, and respect for the setting.

♥ Spark Smiles, Don't Force Laughter

The most effective humor in Impromptu speaking is not about chasing the roar of laughter—it's about sparking the quiet, genuine smile. A smile is universal, disarming, and memorable. When audiences smile, they are leaning in, signaling connection and trust.

Why Smiles Matter

Smiles are a subtle yet powerful form of agreement. They tell the speaker, *"I'm with you."* Even if no one bursts into laughter, the presence of smiles shows that rapport is established. Studies in social psychology confirm that shared smiling increases perceived likability and credibility.

Gentle Humor Over Forced Comedy

Trying too hard to be funny often produces the opposite effect. Forced jokes create tension instead of relief. But gentle humor—an honest observation, a playful twist, a personal anecdote—invites the audience in without pressure. Think less of being a comedian and more of being a companion who helps listeners relax.

Case Studies

Club Example: Asked about pets, a member said, "My dog trained me better than I trained him." The remark drew smiles across the room and set up a warm reflection on patience.

Leadership Example: A mayor addressing budget debates quipped, "I may not balance on a tightrope, but I will balance the budget." The line sparked grins that softened partisan edges and opened ears to the serious message.

Cross-Domain Parallels

In science, micro-interactions between particles create strong bonds; in

~~~~~~~~~~~~~~ •••••••• ~~~~~~~~~~~~~~

"A mediocre speech supported by all the power of delivery is more impressive than the most excellent speech without it."

— **Quintilian**

human interaction, micro-smiles create social bonds.

In nature, primates use play to reduce tension and signal safety; in communication, smiles work the same way.

Practical Application

Aim to spark smiles as your baseline; laughter is a bonus.

Anchor humor in truth, not exaggeration or ridicule.

Leave space for smiles with pauses, instead of rushing ahead.

Humor at its best makes the audience feel good about themselves and comfortable with you. In Impromptu speaking, that is more valuable than any punchline.

Conclusion

Humor in Impromptu speaking is not about telling jokes—it is about connection. By understanding the science of laughter, practicing timing, tone, and tact, and adapting humor to context, speakers can transform uncertain moments into memorable ones. The aim is not forced laughter, but authentic smiles that build trust and rapport. Leaders and communicators who master this approach stand out—not because they perform like comedians, but because they connect like trusted friends. In every Club, contest, or workplace setting, the speaker who can spark smiles in the unscripted moment leaves an impression that lasts far beyond the applause.

While humor can win the room in the moment, it does not define who you are as a speaker. To move from momentary success to lasting recognition, you must cultivate something deeper: your signature style. This is where survival ends, and shine begins.

JOURNAL
Write it Down Before It Escapes!

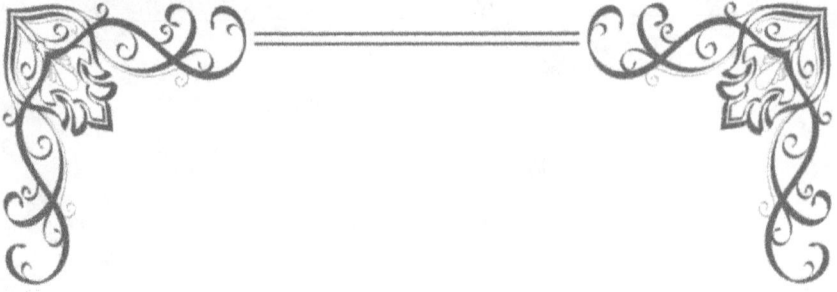

Chapter 18

Your Signature Style: From Survival to Shine

Look out for...

117) Style is not a fixed inheritance; it is a crafted discipline.

118) Self-awareness is the raw material of style creation.

119) Establishing your "style destination" is the first step in creating your style.

120) Without it, style becomes whatever habits happen to form.

121) With it, style becomes a crafted tool of influence.

122) Creating your signature style is not passive discovery—it is intentional design.

123) Not all styles are equally effective.

Humor, as we explored in the previous chapter, is an external tool—a way to connect instantly, lighten the moment, and win the audience's trust. But humor alone does not define you as a speaker. This chapter shifts the focus inward. Here, we examine the development of your *signature style*—not merely identifying it, but *creating it intentionally*. Style is not a fixed inheritance; it is a crafted discipline. The goal is to establish where you want to be, identify where you are, and then plot a practical path between the two points. Humor may win the room, but style makes you remembered.

♥ Creating Your Signature Style: Setting the Goal

Your signature style begins not with accident but with aspiration. Ask: *What kind of impression do I want to leave whenever I speak?* Do I want to be remembered as warm, authoritative, witty, inspiring, relatable, or visionary? Establishing this destination is the first step in creating your style. Developing your signature style must be intentional.

"First, establish where you want to be." — This is the anchor of style creation.

Why Vision Matters

A clear vision prevents drift. Without it, style becomes whatever habits happen to form. With it, style becomes a crafted tool of influence.

Case Study

Professional Example: A leader who wanted to be remembered as approachable began modeling her answers with warmth and stories. Over time, her "approachable authority" became her brand.

♥ Identifying Where You Are

Self-awareness is the raw material of style creation. Record yourself answering Impromptu questions. Seek peer feedback. Note your natural pace,

~~~~~~~~~~~~~~ •••••••• ~~~~~~~~~~~~~~

Impromptu stories must be trimmed because the 'devil" is in the detail. Blame brevity on the lack of time."

— Doctor Perspective™

tone, and gestures. Do you tend to ramble, speak too softly, or default to filler words? Do you show vocal variety or monotone delivery?

"Second, identify where you are." — Honest assessment is the mirror in which true growth begins.

Practical Tools

Recording Exercise: Watch yourself on video. Write down three strengths and three weaknesses.

Feedback Grid: Ask peers to rate you on clarity, confidence, vocal variety, warmth, and presence.

Self-Reflection: What part of your delivery feels forced versus natural?

Case Study

Club Example: A speaker discovered her habit of speaking too quickly. Identifying this weakness allowed her to slow down and add gravitas.

♥ Plotting the Path Between

Once you know your destination and current location, the work is to connect them with deliberate steps.

"Third... plot a practical path between the two points." — Growth is intentional, not accidental.

The Style Ladder (Mediocrity → Excellence)

Survival: Just answering the question.

Awareness: Recognizing habits (tone, rhythm, word choice).

Adjustment: Fixing weaknesses (monotone, filler words).

Expansion: Experimenting with humor, storytelling, rhetorical tools.

Mastery: Owning a distinctive, flexible style audiences recognize.

Case Studies

Toastmasters Example: A monotone speaker who systematically added vocal variety became dynamic and memorable.

Workplace Example: An attorney who was overly aggressive practiced empathetic phrasing, transforming her style into persuasive authority.

Leadership Example: A pastor who once rambled trained himself to structure answers around one story and one lesson, becoming both clear and inspiring.

♥ The Non-Negotiables of a Winning Style

Not all styles are equally effective. Some elements are optional—humor, storytelling, analogy. But some are bare minimum requirements of excellence. Without them, style collapses into mediocrity.

Non-Negotiables

Vocal Variety: Flat tone is never memorable. Vary pitch, pace, and volume to hold attention.

Clarity: Even the most colorful style fails if ideas are muddled.

Presence: Style without presence is decoration without foundation.

Authenticity: Refinement is essential, but faking destroys trust. Stay true to your character while polishing your delivery.

Cross-Domain Parallels

In athletics, every sprinter has a different form, but all must meet the basics of strength, balance, and speed.

In music, each instrument has its own sound, but all require rhythm and tuning.

◊ ♦ ◊ ♦ ◊— ✢ — ✢—◊ ♦ ◊ ♦ ◊— ✢ — ✢—◊ ♦ ◊ ♦ ◊

Whatever is true, whatever is noble, whatever is right, whatever is pure, whatever is lovely, whatever is admirable—if anything is excellent or praiseworthy—think about such things.

Philippians 4:8

Conclusion

Creating your signature style is not passive discovery—it is intentional design. By establishing where you want to be, identifying where you are, and plotting the path between, you move from survival to shine. Along that path, you refine voice, rhythm, and presence. You adopt the non-negotiables—vocal variety, clarity, presence, authenticity—that guarantee effectiveness. The result is not just a style you "happen to have," but one you have created with purpose. That creation becomes your calling card, ensuring that every unscripted response carries your unmistakable mark of excellence.

Humor connects and style distinguishes, but the journey is not complete until you embrace the larger call: to live as a lifetime dominator. The final chapter is not about techniques or tactics—it is about commitment, vision, and stepping into every unscripted moment as an opportunity to lead.

JOURNAL
Write it Down Before It Escapes!

Chapter 19

Final Call to Action: Becoming a Lifetime Dominator

Look out for...

124) *Prepared speeches are rare; Impromptu moments are constant*

125) *The call to action is not abstract; it is lived.*

126) *I know each question is my chance to shine.*

127) *Impromptu mastery is not just a skill; it is a gift to the world.*

128) *Humor connects, style distinguishes, preparation steadies, and presence inspires.*

129) *In communication, Impromptu dominators are catalysts for progress.*

130) *The call is clear: become a lifetime dominator.*

The journey of Impromptu speaking does not end with contests, clubs, or workplace encounters. It extends into every arena of life. This chapter is the rallying cry—the invitation to live as a ***Lifetime Dominator***, someone who transforms every unscripted moment into an opportunity for influence, encouragement, and leadership.

♥ The Call to Mastery

Every skill in this book—from mental toolboxes to humor, from recovery strategies to signature style—has pointed toward one purpose: equipping you to think, speak, and dominate in 15 seconds or less. The call now is not to stop, but to continue mastering.

Why Mastery Matters

Prepared speeches are rare; Impromptu moments are constant. Life's most pivotal conversations are unscripted: a chance encounter, a crisis briefing, a hallway question, a child's tough query. Mastery of the unscripted means mastery of influence.

Case Studies

Professional Example: A manager, once terrified of questions, became the "go-to voice" in meetings through consistent practice.

Personal Life: A father who learned to pause and answer his children thoughtfully built trust and lifelong openness.

Historical Example: Winston Churchill, known for oratory, also mastered the unscripted press question with sharp wit and gravitas.

Practical Application

Commit to practicing Impromptu as deliberately as any formal presentation.

Treat every question as a gift, not a threat.

~~~~~~~~~~~~~~~ •••••••• ~~~~~~~~~~~~~~

"A word fitly spoken is like apples of gold in a setting of silver."

— Proverbs 25:11

Keep growing—humor, style, presence—until mastery feels natural.

♥ Stories of Transformation

The call to action is not abstract; it is lived. Across clubs, workplaces, and personal lives, individuals who embraced Impromptu practice have experienced transformation.

Testimonials

Club Member: "I joined to survive. Now I thrive. I can answer anything with calm."

Young Professional: "Interviews no longer terrify me. They excite me. I know each question is my chance to shine."

Leader: "Impromptu mastery has made me a better listener, parent, and servant-leader."

These voices remind us that the principles of this book are not theory. They are tested, proven, and life-changing.

♥ A Vision for the Future

The world needs more voices of clarity, courage, and compassion. In an age of noise, those who can respond with wisdom in the moment will shape the future.

Why This Matters Now

Workplaces: Demand agile thinkers who can handle questions with poise.

Communities: Need leaders who can respond authentically, not with rehearsed soundbites.

Families: Long for parents, mentors, and friends who listen and answer with presence.

Impromptu mastery is not just a skill; it is a gift to the world.

"Let your speech always be gracious, seasoned with salt."

— **Colossians 4:6**

♥ Cross-Domain Parallels

In science, catalysts speed transformation. In communication, Impromptu dominators are catalysts for progress.

In nature, seeds sprout quickly when the soil is ready. In society, prepared voices sprout influence when opportunity comes.

♥ Your Marching Orders

A call to action must end with clarity. Here are your marching orders as you close this book:

Keep Practicing: Join or form an Impromptu Speech Club. Make practice a habit, not an event.

Mentor Others: Pass on what you know. Each new dominator strengthens the movement.

Expand Horizons: Use humor, style, recovery, and presence not only in clubs or contests but in boardrooms, classrooms, pulpits, and homes.

Stand Ready: Treat every Impromptu question as divine appointment—an invitation to shine.

♥ The Final Rallying Cry

This book began with a spark: the possibility of dominating the first 15 seconds. It now ends with a flame: the vision of a lifetime of Impromptu influence. Humor connects, style distinguishes, preparation steadies, and presence inspires. The call is clear: *become a lifetime dominator*. Step into every moment, every question, every challenge—not with fear, but with readiness.

When your name is called, when the question comes, when the silence begs to be filled—rise. Think. Speak. Dominate. **Always.**

※※※※※※※※※※—✿—✿—※※※※※※※※※※

"Whatever you consciously conceive and ardently believe, you will inevitably achieve!"

— Doctor Perspective™

JOURNAL
You own this book.
How much of its treasures have you owned?

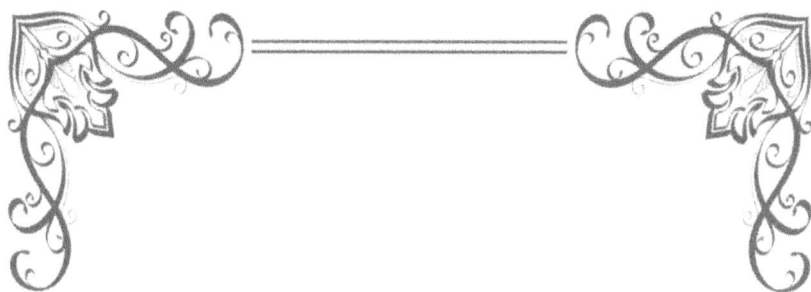

Appendix A

Impromptu Speaking and LCGL's SWAT

In the preceding nineteen chapters, no emphasis has been placed on the importance of Impromptu speaking in the life of the believer in Jesus Christ who is committed to carrying out the Great Commission (Matthew 28:19–20). I have therefore reserved this section to emphasize that almost all of the principles taught in this book are applicable to believers when witnessing for Jesus.

Leaders Communicating God's Love Inc.

I have the distinct pleasure of being the founder and temporary leader of Leaders Communicating God's Love, Inc. (LCGL). LCGL was founded on December 15, 2023, by a group of people who are proud to be Toastmasters and even prouder to be believers in Jesus Christ. Membership was soon extended to any believer in Jesus Christ, regardless of denominational affiliation. LCGL is an interdenominational ministry.

Spiritual Warfare Assertiveness Training

The flagship component of LCGL's ministry is Spiritual Warfare Assertiveness Training (SWAT). Our mantra is "Building Believers for Battle."

SWAT derives its relevance from the Great Commission (Matthew 28:19–20). The life of Jesus on earth shows, among other things, the emphasis he placed on training. He spent three years teaching and training his disciples to become disciple-makers. Yet even after three years of intense, hands-on, live-in training, as Jesus approached the climax of his ministry on earth, all his disciples abandoned him (Matthew 26:56; Mark 14:50; John 16:32). Peter, the most outspoken and proactive of the disciples, denied even knowing Jesus three times—then the rooster crowed.

The Greatest Ever Transfer of Authority

Because Adam chose to disobey God and obey the devil, at that moment he surrendered his God-given power, authority, and dominion to the devil. From that moment, the defeated devil has been (within God's sovereign allowance) legally wielding on earth authority that God had given to man (cf. Genesis 3; Romans 5:12). Jesus's sacrificial death on Calvary's cross in the place of condemned sinners was a major turning point in reclaiming from the devil the authority ceded by man (Colossians 2:15; Matthew 28:18). There is coming a day when he will be completely stripped of all his deceptively acquired authority and will be assigned to hell for all eternity (Revelation 20:10; Matthew 25:41).

Until that time, the devil's mission is to deceive and to convince as many humans as possible to join him in hell (John 8:44; Revelation 12:9; 1 Peter 5:8). The mandate given to every believer in Jesus Christ is to reach as many of those people as possible and share the good news of Jesus's rescue plan for their salvation and deliverance (Matthew 28:19–20; Romans 1:16). LCGL is committed to helping believers build for battle through SWAT.

The Believers Spiritual Weapons

Because of the nature of spiritual warfare, we remember that "the weapons of our warfare are not of the flesh but have divine power to destroy strongholds" (2 Corinthians 10:4, ESV). And "we do not wrestle against flesh and blood, but against the rulers, against the authorities, against the cosmic powers over this present darkness, against the spiritual forces of evil in the heavenly places" (Ephesians 6:10–12, ESV).

The devil and his forces constantly oppose God. As a created being, the devil is no match for God. Yet Adam's sin drew humanity into an ongoing battle for our souls. In Matthew 28:19–20, God clearly states his desire that all people be discipled to obey Jesus' teaching. The devil, on the other hand, works to turn as many people as possible to rebel against God, thereby declaring allegiance to him and sealing their destiny in hell, which was prepared for the devil and his angels (Matthew 25:41). It is also God's expressed desire that his kingdom expand on earth through disciple-making—a process to which LCGL is fully committed.

Advanced Communication Techniques

To build believers for battle, LCGL teaches advanced communication techniques that belong in the disciple-maker's toolkit. Everything in this book is relevant to SWAT, and of course there is more for those who choose to participate in Spiritual Warfare Assertiveness Training. Our website is myLCGL.com; there you will find answers to most questions, and you can contact an LCGL mentor for next steps.

Every Disciple-Maker Should Join a Toastmasters Club

Finally, while Toastmasters International— to whom this book is dedicated— is not a Christian organization, it welcomes everyone, including Christians. I do not know a better organization for every believer in Jesus Christ to join with the intent of developing and honing their leadership and communication skills—both essential in the disciple-maker's toolkit.

Thank you for journeying with me through **Think... Speak... Dominate in 15 Seconds or Less!** May God's goodness and mercy run you down and overtake you, in Jesus' name. Amen!

Appendix B

Bibliography & Recommended Additional Reading

Neuroscience / Psychology

Hickok, Gregory, and David Poeppel. 2007. "The Cortical Organization of Speech Processing." *Nature Reviews Neuroscience* 8(5): 393–402. Why it matters: Dual-stream model of speech—**ventral (comprehension)** and **dorsal (sensorimotor mapping)**—a backbone for how speech/listening are organized in the brain.

Indefrey, Peter, and Willem J. M. Levelt. 2004. "The Spatial and Temporal Signatures of Word Production Components." *Cognition* 92(1–2): 101–144. Why it matters: Meta-analysis mapping **timing** and **locations** from concept → lemma → phonology → articulation; supports rapid message planning.

Indefrey, Peter. 2011. "The Spatial and Temporal Signatures of Word Production Components: A Critical Update." *Frontiers in Psychology* 2: 255.
Why it matters: Ten-year update refining stage timings/regions—useful for speaking under tight time windows.

Phelps, Elizabeth A., and Joseph E. LeDoux. 2005. "Contributions of the Amygdala to Emotion Processing: From Animal Models to Human Behavior." *Neuron* 48(2): 175–187.
Why it matters: Definitive review on **amygdala & fear**—grounds fight/flight, stage fright, "fear circuits."

Dickerson, Sally S., and Margaret E. Kemeny. 2004. "Acute Stressors and Cortisol Responses: A Theoretical Integration and Synthesis of Laboratory Research." *Psychological Bulletin* 130(3): 355–391.
Why it matters: Landmark meta-analysis: **public-speaking/social-evaluative threat** reliably elevates **cortisol**.

Tillfors, Maria, Tomas Furmark, Mikael Fischer, et al. 2002. "Cerebral Blood Flow During Anticipation of Public Speaking in Social Phobia: A PET Study." *Biological Psychiatry* 52(11): 1113–1119.
Why it matters: Anticipation of public speaking activates anxiety circuitry—evidence behind exposure practice.

Tillfors, Maria, Tomas Furmark, Mats Marteinsdottir, et al. 2001. "Cerebral Blood Flow in Subjects with Social Phobia During Stressful Speaking Tasks: A PET Study." *American Journal of Psychiatry* 158(8): 1220–1226.
Why it matters: Shows brain differences **during** public-speaking stress.

Beilock, Sian L., and Thomas H. Carr. 2005. "When High-Powered People Fail: Working Memory and 'Choking under Pressure.'" *Psychological Science* 16(2): 101–105.
Why it matters: Pressure **overloads working memory**, degrading performance—transfers to speaking under time pressure.

Baddeley, Alan D. 2000. "The Episodic Buffer: A New Component of Working Memory?" *Trends in Cognitive Sciences* **4(11): 417–423.**
Why it matters: Introduces the **episodic buffer**—helps justify concise, "chunked" messaging.

McGurk, Harry, and John MacDonald. 1976. "Hearing Lips and Seeing Voices." *Nature* **264(5588): 746–748.**
Why it matters: The **McGurk effect**—visuals can change what listeners "hear." Supports your coaching on articulation and presence.

Rhetoric / Communication & Writing

Aristotle. 2007. *On Rhetoric: A Theory of Civic Discourse.* 2nd ed. Translated by George A. Kennedy. Oxford: Oxford University Press.
Quintilian. 1920–1922. *Institutio Oratoria.* Translated by H. E. Butler. Loeb Classical Library. Cambridge, MA: Harvard University Press.
Shakespeare, William. *Hamlet.* Folger Shakespeare Library edition (updated). Washington, DC: Folger, 2012.
Strunk, William Jr., and **E. B. White.** 2000. *The Elements of Style.* 4th ed. New York: Longman.
Zinsser, William. 2006. *On Writing Well.* Revised and expanded ed. New York: Harper Perennial.

Scripture Permissions & Credits

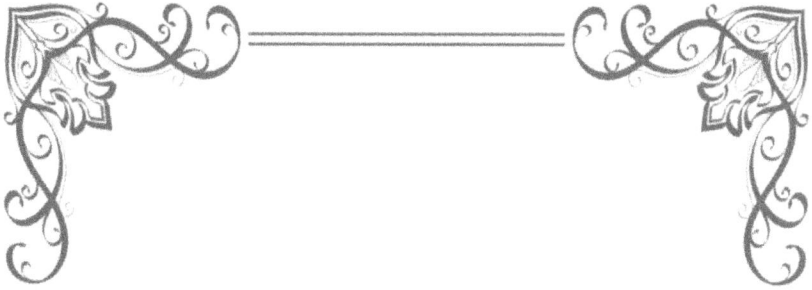

Appendix C

Attributions

Following is a list of Quotes attributed to authors and speakers other than Dr. Godfrey E. McAllister, aka **Doctor Perspective™**.

1. "I never could make a good Impromptu speech without several hours to prepare it." — Mark Twain.

2. "If I am to speak for ten minutes, I need a week for preparation; if an hour, I am ready now."
   — Woodrow Wilson (1918).

3. "Where observation is concerned, chance favours only the prepared mind." — Louis Pasteur, inaugural lecture, 7 Dec 1854. (Oxford Reference)

4. "Plans are worthless, but planning is everything."
   — Dwight D. Eisenhower (1957).

5. "Preparation, I have often said, is rightly two-thirds of any venture." — Amelia Earhart, *Last Flight* (1937). (Project Gutenberg)

6. "Practice is nine-tenths." — Ralph Waldo Emerson, *The Conduct of Life* (1860).

7. "No plan of operations extends with certainty beyond the first encounter with the enemy." — Helmuth von Moltke (the Elder). (Quote Investigator)

8. "I have made this longer than usual because I have not had time to make it shorter." — Blaise Pascal, *Provincial Letters* (1657).

9. "Brevity is the soul of wit." — William Shakespeare, *Hamlet* II.ii.

10. "Speak clearly, if you speak at all; carve every word before you let it fall." — Oliver Wendell Holmes, Sr., *Poetry: A Metrical Essay*.

11. "Omit needless words." — William Strunk Jr. & E. B. White, *The Elements of Style* (Rule 17).

12. "Clutter is the disease of American writing." — William Zinsser, *On Writing Well*.

13. "The right word may be effective, but no word was ever as effective as a rightly timed pause." — Mark Twain, *Mark Twain's Speeches* (1923 ed.). (twainquotes.com)

14. "Speak the speech, I pray you, as I pronounced it to you, trippingly on the tongue." — William Shakespeare, *Hamlet* III.ii.

15. "Suit the action to the word, the word to the action." — William Shakespeare, *Hamlet* III.ii.

16. "Give every man thy ear, but few thy voice." — William Shakespeare, *Hamlet* I.iii.

17. "Speak when you're angry and you'll make the best speech you'll ever regret." — Proverbial (earliest attributions not to Ambrose Bierce; misattributed).

18. "Be sincere, be brief, be seated." — Common speaking adage, often credited to FDR (attribution uncertain).

19. "Only the prepared speaker deserves to be confident." — Dale Carnegie, *The Quick and Easy Way to Effective Speaking*.

20. "All the great speakers were bad speakers at first."
— Ralph Waldo Emerson, *The Conduct of Life* (1860).

21. "I would not hesitate to assert that a mediocre speech supported by all the power of delivery will be more impressive than the best speech unaccompanied by such power."
— Quintilian, *Institutio Oratoria* XI.3.

22. "Asked what was the chief element in oratory, Demosthenes is said to have answered: delivery; and when asked the second, he replied: delivery; and the third, delivery."
— Quintilian reporting Demosthenes, *Institutio Oratoria* XI.3.

23. "It is not enough to know what we ought to say; we must also say it as we ought." — Aristotle, *Rhetoric* III.1.

24. "If it is possible to cut a word out, always cut it out."
— George Orwell, "Politics and the English Language."

25. "What is written without effort is generally read without pleasure." — Samuel Johnson (earliest solid evidence), *Quote Investigator*.

26. "Proper words, in proper places, make the true definition of a style." — Jonathan Swift, *A Letter to a Young Gentleman, Lately Enter'd into Holy Orders* (1720/21).

27. "Once more: speak clearly, if you speak at all; / Carve every word before you let it fall;" — Oliver Wendell Holmes, Sr., *The Poetical Works of Oliver Wendell Holmes* ("The Deacon's Masterpiece").

28. "The secret of being a bore is to tell everything."
— Voltaire, *Sept Discours en Vers sur l'Homme* (1738).

29. "A soft answer turns away wrath, but a harsh word stirs up anger." — Proverbs 15:1 (ESV).

30. "Let every person be quick to hear, slow to speak, slow to anger." — James 1:19 (ESV).

31. Whatever is true, whatever is noble, whatever is right, whatever is pure, whatever is lovely, whatever is admirable—if anything is excellent or praiseworthy—think about such things. — Philippians 4:8 (ESV)

32. *"The Lord is my light and my salvation; whom shall I fear? The Lord is the stronghold of my life; of whom shall I be afraid?"* — Psalm 27:1 (ESV)

33. *"Death and life are in the power of the tongue, and those who love it will eat its fruits."* — Proverbs 18:21 (ESV)

Quotes Attributed to Dr. Godfrey E. McAllister

1. "A well-timed pause is the secret sauce of humor." — Doctor Perspective™
2. "An evasive or defensive answer erodes credibility." — Doctor Perspective™
3. "As it is in the animal kingdom, students instinctively read posture." — Doctor Perspective™
4. "Audiences perceive spontaneity as authenticity." — Doctor Perspective™
5. "Audiences respond instinctively to shifts in volume, pace, and pitch." — Doctor Perspective™
6. "Brevity signals clarity and respect." — Doctor Perspective™
7. "Collect tough questions you've faced—or fear facing... and conquer them." — Doctor Perspective™
8. "Energy matters as much as content does. Energize your content," — Doctor Perspective™
9. "Fear thrives in the absence of structure." — Doctor Perspective™
10. "Flexibility is the universal key." — Doctor Perspective™
11. "Framework fluency is what makes you look not rehearsed, but responsive." — Doctor Perspective™
12. "Frameworks must respect the setting." — Doctor Perspective™
13. "Gestures are not accessories. They are essential" — Doctor Perspective™
14. "Good transitions either signal direction, or can be humorously used for misdirection." — Doctor Perspective™

15. "Make practice a habit, not an event."
— Doctor Perspective™
16. "Master the unscripted and you master the moment."
— Doctor Perspective™
17. "Naming your dominant fear is the first step in loosening its grip." — Doctor Perspective™
18. "Not every curveball deserves a full swing."
— Doctor Perspective™
19. "Not every question is neutral. Some are like a loaded gun"
— Doctor Perspective™
20. "Pausing before the punchline builds anticipation."
— Doctor Perspective™
21. "Silence filled with calm is interpreted as thoughtfulness, not weakness." — Doctor Perspective™
22. "Some soared. Some stumbled. All grew."
— Doctor Perspective™
23. "Speed without wisdom is reckless."
— Doctor Perspective™
24. "The difference that sealed the deal was not data, but delivery." — Doctor Perspective™
25. The human voice is the most flexible instrument on earth. Use it. — Doctor Perspective™
26. "The pause is not hesitation—it is orchestration." —
Doctor Perspective™
27. "The question is your foundation." — Doctor Perspective™
28. "The safest humor is self-directed, not self-deprecating."
— Doctor Perspective™
29. "The silence itself becomes a vocal tool."
— Doctor Perspective™
30. "Theory is only as powerful as practice."
— Doctor Perspective™
31. "Your first defense is composure." — Doctor Perspective™
32. "Whatever you consciously conceive and ardently believe, you will inevitably achieve." — Doctor Perspective™

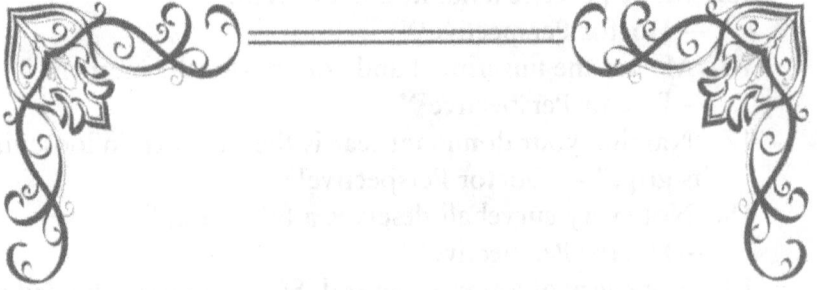

About the Author

I am Godfrey Ezekiel McAllister. I have worn many hats. I have experienced life's joys and challenges across multiple continents. I am confident that my wide range of exposures, experiences, and even experiments played a significant role in my deciding to trademark my name –

Doctor Perspective™, along with my mantra, "The only thing over which you have complete control is your perspective."™

Born in Guyana, I spent most of my life in Jamaica. Now I live in the United States. My journey has been one of continuous learning, growth, and a deep passion for helping others unlock their full potential.

Confirmed Stutterer "Converted"

Life is full of paradoxes. Upon reflection, my story probably begins during my early adolescent life when I was a confirmed person who has a stutter. In Guyana, we called it, stammer. I could barely utter two words without repeating at least one of them. I was a social outcast. With a head that was disproportionate to the rest of my body, my peers mockingly called me "big-head, stammering Mac". And what that meant is that girls despised me. That could have been an end-of-life event for a young teenager.

How I overcame stuttering to become a world-class speaker will be the subject for a future book. And if you invite me to speak at a special event, remind me to share that story. But I overcame stammering, although, today I still occasionally 'stutter'.

Fascinated by Power of Communication

From my early days as a guidance counselor to my record-breaking achievements in the life insurance industry, the power of effective communication has always fascinated me. As someone who has won multiple public speaking competitions, I have seen how quick thinking and clear communication can make a difference in people's lives and inspire change.

My passion for Impromptu speaking led me to join Toastmasters International in 2001. I became the first Distinguished Toastmaster in the Caribbean and played an inspirational role in establishing a new District that serves 28 countries. Through this experience, I discovered the immense potential of Impromptu speaking as a tool for personal and professional growth.

Life-long Learner

As a lifelong learner, I have sought to expand my knowledge and skills across various domains. The major of my Bachelor's degree is Theology, supplemented by a minor in Psychology. My Master's degree is in Theocentric Counseling. My related published thesis is "You've Got All It Takes to Succeed". My Ph.D. is in Human Relations, specializing in Consumer-Provider Relations. My related published thesis is "Winning the War? Consumer Survival in a Free Market Economy"

Among my earned professional designations are the Chartered Life Underwriter (CLU); the Chartered Financial Consultant (Ch.F.C.); and the Distinguished Toastmaster (DTM).

Sales & Marketing Professional

Apart from two years spent as a Guidance Counsellor with Ministry of Education in Jamaica, most of my professional life was spent in the Life Insurance Industry in which I enjoyed some distinctions.

I qualified for the prestigious Million Dollar Round Table in my first three months in the industry. I was the first person in Jamaica to qualify for, and attend the ultimately prestigious Top of the Table section of the International Million Dollar Round Table. Along with that came breaking all available records at Life of Jamaica. At American Life Insurance Company (ALICo), I was #1 in Jamaica in my first year in the field of Personal Accident Insurance Sales. In my second year I was #1 in the Caribbean. In my 3rd year, I was #1 in ALICo's world of over 60 countries. I retained the #1 world-wide Producer title for seven consecutive years, each year breaking my own record. Perhaps my greatest achievement in the Insurance Industry s that 40 years later, the block of business that I created is still "in force". This is testament to the truth that a needs-oriented sale that is supported by efficient service is self-sustainable and self-perpetuating.

My Perspective on Impromptu Speaking

Throughout my professional pursuits, I have developed a deep understanding of the human psyche and the dynamics of interpersonal relationships. My diverse roles as a Counselor, Consumer Advocate, Supreme Court Mediator, TV and Radio Host, Politician, Super Service Provider (SSP), and Minister of the Gospel of Jesus Christ have all further enriched my perspective on the importance of effective communication.

Motivation for Writing This book

It is through these experiences that I realized the need for a comprehensive guide to Impromptu speaking. It was in my Toastmasters Club that my appetite for Impromptu speaking excellence was triggered. It soon became obvious that my Impromptu speaking skills were being tested, but not taught. When compared to the excellent detailed training that was accorded the "prepared speech", the contrast was stark.

I wrote **Think... Speak... Dominate in 15 Seconds or Less!** to share my knowledge and skills with anyone who wants to become better at speaking spontaneously. Whether you are a business professional, student, or simply someone looking to enhance your communication skills, this book is for you.

It provides the tools and confidence you need to navigate any speaking situation with ease and finesse.

What You Will Learn

In this book, I delve into the psychology behind rapid cognition, the importance of building a solid knowledge base, and the strategies for organizing your thoughts on the spot. I also explore the power of storytelling, the art of reading your audience, and the techniques for handling tough questions and controversial topics. Through practical examples, real-life anecdotes, and proven methods, I aim to demystify the process of Impromptu speaking. This will help readers unlock their full potential as effective communicators.

My Goal

My goal in writing this book is to empower individuals to embrace the challenges and opportunities of Impromptu speaking. I hope to inspire you to become a confident, articulate, and persuasive speaker in any situation. I believe that the ability to communicate effectively is not just a skill, but a superpower that can transform your life and shape the world around you.

I hope that **Think... Speak... Dominate in 15 Seconds or Less!** will serve as a catalyst for personal and professional growth, and help you unleash ability to dominate every challenge.

Thank you

Thank you for allowing the opportunity and privilege of helping you become the best that you can be.

This is just the beginning. I am at your service.

The World-wide Impromptu Speaking Empowerment (WISE) virtual community has been established with you in mind. Visit us at

https://TheWISEworld.org

. there you will find all the information you need. Membership validation will be required only if you would like to attend one of our events at a discounted rate. Otherwise, you are welcome to share in everything that is available in our virtual community.

Please join our community and stay connected!

www.ingramcontent.com/pod-product-compliance
Lightning Source LLC
Chambersburg PA
CBHW060306100426
42742CB00011B/1883